PRAISE FOR
SOCIAL SELLING

'A Network gives you Reach... but a Community gives you Power. It's time to stop making excuses and start bringing in personal social skills to the digital world. The authors not only understand this critical issue, they give you the tools to make it happen.' **Ted Rubin, Social Marketing Strategist, keynote speaker, and CMO of Brand Innovators, @tedrubin**

'Finally a social selling book that is full of meat, not fluff and buzzwords! A must-read for the sales-focused organization and its team.' **Robert M Caruso, fondalo.com, @fondalo**

'Hits on every single ideology that leaders at all levels need to hear and understand in order to keep their sales and marketing teams relevant in the digital age. The terminology used in this book is more than just the future of business, it is the now of business, and should serve as a wake-up call before it's too late.' **Jack Kosakowski, Global Head of B2B Social Sales Strategy, Creation Agency, @jackkosakowski1**

'Tim Hughes is top of the class of #SocialSelling teachers and practitioners. He is unique amongst #SocialSales influencers in that he actually uses social every day to sell more with less work. I loved reading *Social Selling* because it comes from a true salesperson who works in the business trenches every day. Run, don't walk, to buy your copy of *Social Selling*, to start selling Better, Smarter, Faster, the Social Selling Way.' **Jon Ferrara, pioneer of #CRM, #SocialSelling, CEO of Nimble, founder of GoldMine, @Jon_ferrara**

'*Social Selling* is a timely, relevant, authoritative how-to guide for any salesperson who doesn't want to get left behind. The authors have written a fierce book for salespeople who want to win in today's new, hyper-connected, hyper-social economy.' **Jim Keenan, CEO, A Sales Guy Inc, author of *Not Taught*, @keenan**

'The biggest problem with social selling is that most people confuse what it should really mean to their business. Using social media as part of your business is one thing, but following the practical advice of this book is what most businesses need if they want to see a return on their social efforts. Having had the chance to not only read the book, but to follow Tim Hughes across social for many years, I put this book at the top of the pile when it comes to useful reads on this topic.' **Daniel Newman, CEO of Broadsuite Media Group, *Forbes* contributor and author, @danielnewmanUV**

'*Social Selling* sets the scene beautifully, explaining why, in a nutshell, sales is having to evolve for the first time in hundreds of years, thanks to the rise of social media and the always-mobile customer. But this isn't a book about the past; Hughes and Reynolds eloquently explain the future of sales with real takeaways, practical advice and detailed explanations. This book isn't about how to leverage tools to bend the will of the prospective customer: it is about how to build real trust, authority and influence in a world that can see through manipulative sales practices in a heartbeat.' **Stewart Rogers, Director, Marketing Technology, VB Insight, @TheRealSJR**

'*Social Selling* is a masterwork! At long last, the how-to manual that every sales leader has been hoping for. Pray your competition doesn't read this before you do!' **Ted Coiné, speaker, author, founder of OPENfor.business, @tedcoine**

Social Selling
Techniques to influence buyers and changemakers

Tim Hughes and Matt Reynolds

Kogan Page

LONDON PHILADELPHIA NEW DELHI

First published in Great Britain and the United States in 2016 by Kogan Page Limited

2nd Floor, 45 Gee Street	1518 Walnut Street, Suite 900	4737/23 Ansari Road
London EC1V 3RS	Philadelphia PA 19102	Daryaganj
United Kingdom	USA	New Delhi 110002
		India

www.koganpage.com

© Tim Hughes and Matt Reynolds, 2016

ISBN   978 0 7494 7801 8
E-ISBN   978 0 7494 7802 5

British Library Cataloguing-in-Publication Data

A CIP record for this book is available from the British Library.

Library of Congress Cataloging-in-Publication Data

Names: Hughes, Tim, 1965– author. | Reynolds, Matt, 1974– author.
Title: Social selling : techniques to influence buyers and changemakers / Tim Hughes and Matt Reynolds.
Description: London ; Philadelphia : Kogan Page, 2016. | Includes bibliographical references and index.
Identifiers: LCCN 2016016198 (print) | LCCN 2016024636 (ebook) | ISBN 9780749478018 (paperback) | ISBN 9780749478025 (ebook)
Subjects: LCSH: Selling–Social aspects. | Sales management. | Internet marketing. | Social media. | Customer relations. | BISAC: BUSINESS & ECONOMICS / Sales & Selling.
Classification: LCC HF5438.25 .H8656 2016 (print) | LCC HF5438.25 (ebook) | DDC 658.85–dc23

Typeset by SPi Global
Print production managed by Jellyfish
Printed and bound by CPI Group (UK) Ltd, Croydon, CR0 4YY

CONTENTS

Bonus supporting resources are available at the following url (please scroll to the bottom of the web page and complete the form to access these):

www.koganpage.com/socialselling

Introduction to social selling

The idea of social selling always sounds appealing. All you have to do to sell on social media is log in, find opportunities, and close deals. Easy, right?

Moreover, the question 'why should you do social selling?' seems like it has an obvious answer. In reality though, the standard answer of 'it's a new, good way to find leads' is misleading. As we shall go on to explain, the reality is that over time social selling will become the only way that B2B (Business to Business) selling can be done at all.

Traditional interrupt selling or marketing

Sales has traditionally worked by having the salesperson 'interrupt' a C-level executive.

In organizations (especially in the United States) the highest-level people have job titles such as Chief Executive Officer (CEO), Chief Financial Officer (CFO), etc. It is these people that are often called, collectively, C-level. It is assumed that they all sit together on one floor of a corporation and this is often called the C-suite. In this book, when we talk about selling or marketing at the highest level in an organization, we will use the term C-level.

The salesperson would traditionally have to fight through the gate-keeper (personal assistant, secretary or voice mail) to eventually have a conversation with that C-level executive. From there the sales-person would sell an idea into the business. In order for the deal to work, that idea would promise a vision that would look to solve some problem that was causing pain to the business. The idea would then be nurtured into strategy, and from there into implementation. Sales was a partnership, that partnership being formed at the top level of the organization.

The problem with the classical sales approach is that the salesperson naturally brings bias into the organization. Although salespeople selling complex solutions will act in a way that's like a consultant, their agenda is to sell what they want to sell – perhaps more properly put as 'in a position to sell' – and that solution might not be exactly what the business needs.

This has been a historic fault in how businesses buy throughout the whole history of commerce – this method of allowing the C-level exec to be 'sold at' by an external agent will always bring in bias. Businesses accepted this bias and attendant inefficiency because it used to be too difficult to approach the problem in a different way. Having the C-level exec constantly interrupted by salespeople was a good enough way for the business to get its needs met.

However, businesses, like all complex organisms, will tend to find more optimal solutions to problems, and so now businesses are actively evolving to change the way they run the buying process so that this external bias is removed.

Businesses are now finding they achieve better results by asking employees to use social networks to research solutions to problems in a way that removes bias. By going out into the social networks and using the 'hive mind', 'network effect', 'connected economy', and so on, businesses can design solutions for themselves that are as good as those designed by external salespeople, but don't have the problem of bias.

The upshot of this is that the salesperson is being squeezed out of the buying process – or rather being pushed further down the process until such time as they have to be included. That's clearly not ideal for the salesperson, although it does produce better results for the business.

Social selling is a different way of buying

Social selling is a reaction to this change in buyer behaviour. It proposes a way of getting the salesperson back into the buying process so that they can once again control and influence the buying decisions of the business.

This is a very important fact to appreciate. Social selling isn't an opportunity that has come about because social media creates a different way to sell. Social selling is a reaction that has come about because social media creates a different way to buy.

Traditional selling has stopped being effective

What sales organizations have started to feel as this change in buyer behaviour takes hold is that traditional methods of selling have stopped being as effective as they once were. A common symptom is that C-level execs are much harder to reach on the phone than before. This is not a result of society (and hence C-level execs) becoming ruder, it's a result of the fact that the C-level execs would rather listen to information coming up through their business from social networks as opposed to information coming in sideways from salespeople, because ultimately they get a better, less biased/more efficient, result.

Today, the mechanism by which this process works is straightforward. C-level execs generally don't engage on social networks, because typically they are in their mid-40s (at least) and mostly don't 'get the point' of social networks. We often get the comment from C-level executives that social media is for kids or for posting photos of your lunch. They don't see how that can make a transformational impact to their business.

The changemaker #Changemakers

What they do instead is turn to people in their organization who do get social networks and task them with using their social networking skills and experience to 'ideate' solutions to the business's complex problems. Even if there is no formal top-down decision to use this tactic, a certain type of person lower down in the organization is increasingly taking the initiative to ideate in this way.

We call these individuals lower down in the organization 'change-makers', and they are so important to social selling that we have developed the 'Changemaker Method' as a way of framing our social selling methodology. This methodology describes the path a business must take to transform from one where the market is engaged through classic sales techniques to one where the market is engaged through social sales techniques.

Where do changemakers come from?

To define a changemaker, consider that C-level executives don't just 'pop' into existence. They are gestated and cultivated within businesses as part of their early careers. They are individuals who use talent, drive, experience, skills and charisma to prove themselves within the business, their ultimate goal being to get their feet under a desk in the C-suite offices. They are people who typically 'live to work' as opposed to 'work to live', and are always looking for ways to improve the business. It is likely that you were a changemaker before you reached the senior position you hold in your own business.

A changemaker will either find or be given a problem to fix. For example, they might be asked, 'Can you find out why our phone system keeps cutting people off mid-call?'

You, as a salesperson of (in this example) hosted telephony systems, need to find this person and get them to buy your product in order to fix this problem. Let's look at the process the changemaker uses to solve this problem. Again, we want to look at buyer behaviour, not the behaviour of the salesperson.

Changemakers in action

Today we have a situation where changemakers have left an education system that has been – mostly accidentally – designed along the principles of a connected economy.

Throughout their schooling people who are today in their 20s and 30s have learnt to create ad hoc teams, to connect with people through social media as well as face to face, to bring out the best in themselves and manage out weak spots in teams. They've learnt, essentially, that to do something good, they need to work with groups of people that don't necessarily have affiliations to the classical reporting structure. This is hugely different to how C-level execs in their 40s and older learnt how to operate within business.

Ideation

Today's changemaker solves the problem of 'customer calls keep getting cut off' by going out to their social network and asking, 'Hey, has anyone got any idea what I should do about the phone system at work? It keeps cutting people off!' From there, the network effect kicks in and the information about how to fix the customer's problem comes from within the network. This process is called 'ideation'. It is how the vision of a solution to a problem gets developed.

The changemaker then takes their vision of the solution to the C-level execs for approval. The C-level execs approve the strategy, and provide funds to back it up. The changemaker then needs to implement, which is very easy for them because they can just outsource it to an expert in implementation. Again, that implementation expert will often be selected simply by asking for referrals on the social network.

And that's the scary part for traditional salespeople, because they are almost totally uninvolved in that buying process. They certainly do not get to have a major influence within it. If they're very lucky, they'll work for the selected vendor and get to take the order.

Changemaker persona

So what is the persona of a changemaker? What is it that makes them tick? How do you spot one?

Changemakers will have authority. They may not have it by position, for example by being a vice president (VP), but they do have it, as VPs often turn to them when a decision is needed. We discuss later in the book the need for influence in the digital economy, which is the way that changemakers have authority, online.

It could be argued that changemakers are, in the digital world, the new decision makers. Most C-suite executives don't understand the connected economy, but have probably read an article somewhere that says they need to do something about it. They therefore turn to their trusted changemakers for guidance.

Research by Google dated 5 November 2014, 'Digital Tipping Points for 2015' written by @Tuomisto has the following findings: the C-Suite have final authority on 64 per cent of decisions. But layer on non C-suite decision making and you can see that non-C-suite can influence 81 per cent of purchase decisions (Tuomisto-Inch, 2015). How can that be?

It may be that the C-suite have signed off an overall project budget, but the components of that project are passed/delegated down the organization to 'people in the know'. For example, there might be an overall Customer Experience Transformation project, but the individual software components that make that up are purchased lower down the organization. In addition, in the new world of SaaS/Cloud, software can be switched off as quickly as it's switched on, and there can be very short implementation timeframes, so there may not be a need for traditional IT involvement.

Based on Google's same research of the 'people in the know', 48 per cent of them are 18–34 years old and 24 per cent are 35–44. This is placing B2B enterprise decisions in the hands of 'changemakers'.

Where are changemakers going?

Essentially, tomorrow's C-level execs have emerged from education and gone into commercial life having a very good understanding of how to use a network to ideate solutions to complex problems. Importantly, this ideation happens without bias, and as we said before, bias is a block to efficiency. Now we're in a situation where the C-level exec doesn't have to be interrupted by salespeople anymore because he can just pass problems down to changemakers who very keenly go out and find a solution to the business's problem on social media.

Social selling is all about getting the salesperson back into that process. The theory of 'how' this is done is extremely easy. The changemaker is using their social network to ideate and design the solution, and they do this by creating an ad hoc team of advisors that 'spitball' the problem and come up with an answer.

All the salesperson has to do is get themselves invited into that ad hoc team created by the changemaker. In turn, all that involves is getting the salesperson to a point where they can be discovered and listened to. In this book we will discuss the need for community.

Community is often talked about in the realms of some sort of hippy idealism. We will talk about how community can be used in driving leads, revenue and killing the competition. Sorry if you are looking for a fluffy view of the world, but this is a book about how salespeople can use social to crush their numbers. Hack the buying process.

Hashtag Changemakers – #Changemakers

Becoming a digital organization is going to take change – if you are a changemaker then get in touch using the hashtag #Changemakers and let us know what you are doing.

Buckle up

The book has some pretty radical ideas and methods, but we feel that sales organizations have been the same for the last 50 years. They no longer meet the needs of a modern digital organization. We provide a method that organizations can implement so rather than being an analogue organization with random acts of social, an organization disrupts itself so it meets the needs of a team of social sellers. This journey won't be easy and we have a number of new concepts to grapple with, so buckle up for the ride.

Hacking the buying process

This book has been designed to be a manual; it outlines the changes that have taken place in society due to the connected economy. We also provide practical help to salespeople, sales leaders and marketers on how this connected economy now works and the changes organizations now need to embrace if they are to stay relevant.

With buyers spending more and more time in salespeople avoidance mode, what can you do to leverage this exciting new buying process to your advantage?

Community and tribalism

01

Before we jump in and talk about social and how it can be used to help you create leads, revenue and gain competitive advantage, let's go back in time and discuss community.

Way back in time (it was recorded in 1086 in the Doomsday Book) humans formed into groups and tribes. The objective was survival, living on hunting, fishing and farming. When a crop failed people realized it was better to work together as a team than as individuals. As time went on, people were required to work in jobs that were not related to hunting and gathering, for example, smelting metal for weapons or for horse shoes, made by a blacksmith and fitted to the horse by a farrier.

Even before the introduction of money, people would have bartered their wares. The ploughman would want shoes for his horses and the farrier would want food for his family. The society was based on a common purpose. In a village community, everybody knew their role and worked for the common good. Society expected you to 'add value' for the survival of the tribe.

It wasn't just about completing your role; you might also help out other people. During the harvest, people would work together to make sure the crops were harvested in time. People would also unselfishly make introductions for the common good. Contrary to the view of Darwin that the world is dog-eat-dog, many scientists now believe the human ability to collaborate is what has made us so successful (there's a great link to Keltner's 2012 article at the back of the book).

Today people use sites like TripAdvisor, where you leave your views and recommendations on hotels. The rationale is that you are more likely to book something that a friend has recommended, or book a hotel that a friend of a friend has recommended. The theory is that if you trust friend A, then while you have never met their friend, on the basis that friend A is OK, surely their friends are OK too.

Research conducted by Ipsos Media and Crowdtap in 2014 showed that the recommendations of strangers on such sites have a powerful influence on behaviour (Knoblauch, 2014).

Recently, a friend of mine was intent on taking a destination vacation with his family. He booked 10 days in a motel, thinking that was his best option, but after I had raved about it, thought he would try Airbnb. A search revealed he could get a beautiful private house in the same location as the motel he had chosen for half the price.

But there was a catch. He learned that Airbnb landlords are not obligated to rent their property to anyone who can afford it. Instead, they only approve people they trust.

How does someone who has never met you and lives thousands of miles away come to entrust you, a stranger, with one of their most prized possessions? The answer might be obvious – social media. If you are an Airbnb renter who has never used the service before – and, therefore, has never been rated on the website by a landlord – you are an unknown entity. In order to reduce the risk, the service encourages property owners to do something unusual. They learn how to check you out online via sites like Facebook, LinkedIn, Twitter and company websites. Your public presence, on social media in particular, helps determine whether or not you represent a high risk; the kind of tenant who will ruin their home.

While in the next chapter we discuss how you can create a personal brand, here we discuss how for the B2B (Business to Business) and B2C (Business to Consumer) salesperson, community is now the de facto place to live, work and sell online.

The mistake many people make about communities or tribes is that it's all about the number of people in that tribe. A modern term for that could be followers. Or people often mistake it as market reach. Community isn't that either. The key is that people share amongst themselves for the common good of that community. There are no egos. In our communities on social media, if there are people I think would benefit from my connecting them with each other, I effect that introduction. For example, a friend of mine was setting up a website to help students find jobs. So I introduced her to students that I knew had found work through LinkedIn, which gave her validation of her ideas and strong case studies. It is highly unlikely I will profit from that enterprise, but I will be pleased to see it thrive and maybe I can help my friend and other people. We call it Social Karma.

Communities or tribes have always had leaders. If we continue our ancient history analogy, it could be the lord of the manor or the tribe chief.

The tribal chief had a role to provide leadership, was ceremonial and provided governance but in the majority of cases the community lived and thrived by itself.

Dan Newman (@danielnewmanUV) is CEO of Broadsuite Media Group, a *Forbes* contributor and author of five books. He said to me, 'My definition of community is that your tribe will carry your torch for you; if you carry it yourself you are just a person'.

Having worked in many corporations this can be contradictory to common thinking. Yes I understand that a company has a common purpose as defined by the board of directors and itemized in the annual accounts, but at the shop floor level people have their own agendas. I've worked in teams that have 'knowledge is power' and 'not invented here' attitudes. Where any good idea is immediately stolen and presented as a manager's own. All of this fosters negative feelings. Why would you want to innovate when you don't get the acknowledgement for your efforts and thoughts?

In any company regardless of size there are often more demands on you than hours in the day; you therefore have to decide what is today's priority. You also have to obey the rules, whether this is the corporate culture or to meet the needs of shareholders or regulation. This often 'institutionalizes' the way people think. How many times have we heard 'but we have always done it like that', when we asked people why they are following that particular process?

The big jump that people need to make in the move from corporate thinking to working in the networked or connected economy is that you are working in communities or tribes. Not in a corporate structure. Based on the way communities have thrived since history began, you need to be supportive. This isn't some 'hippy' life construct but a need to allow give and take in that network. Somebody has to smelt the metal, the blacksmith will make the horses' shoes and the farrier will fit them to the horses. If you are not passing on the baton of help (adding value, as people often call it) then there is no community. People are hungry for real conversations and real relationships. It just has to be authentic, genuine and sincere.

If you are reading this, we hope you are one of the vendors and services providers attempting to trigger and engage in online digital conversations, within your target market segments. This will increase awareness, reputation, thought leadership, online connections and lead origination.

So what? You only get out of community what you put in and if you are taking and not giving in at least equal quantity then you won't grow your follower base, your community and you won't get to create the leads and revenue you want. For example, a friend of mine offers GooglePlus training, and when I come across people who need training in this area, I connect them. When he gets an inbound from me, he tweets a blog we wrote together. This gives me amplification over his network, which is generally a different type of person to my usual follower, and allows for cross-pollination of networks.

Another example is where a contact sent me a LinkedIn message about a LinkedIn group he has created for people who train others on LinkedIn. Michael (let's call him that) is going to gain, as he will get advice from some of the best LinkedIn trainers like us. But he knows that to gain that knowledge he also needs to share his own. In the world of connected networks your competitor is also your friend. This is often called 'Frenemies'; the building of mutual trust and respect across the connected economy.

The struggle people often have is that when you are working in a network you need to shake off the shackles of corporate thinking. When you get online you will find connection requests and you will be followed by people you don't know. People (whom you have never met and are unlikely to meet) will make decisions about you based on your social profiles. If your LinkedIn profile or Twitter account is stuffed with corporate speak, then people will see you as a corporate suit. As startup advisor, keynote speaker and social selling evangelist Jill Rowley (@jill_rowley) often says, 'If you suck offline, you're going to suck more online'. More on personal branding and how to set up a social profile can be found in Chapter 2.

But this journey from corporate thinking to social karma is not something that most people will be able to grapple with and come to terms with overnight. Tim thinks it took him 18 months to come to terms with it. However, once he realized he needed to relax and be himself, he 'found his voice' on social media.

This book isn't a 'self-help' book but we do want you to realize that getting online and working in the connected society isn't about pressing a button and automatically being switched over. It takes time to change and adapt your thinking.

Social is a maturing science. This book does not hold all the answers as social will change as we find new ways of using it to drive profit and competitive advantage. One way to look at community is based on social proximity. This is a relationship-based approach of assigning opportunities and accounts based on the social connections and engagement of your sales team. In other words, the salesperson most closely connected to and engaged with the buyer through friends and professional networks owns the opportunity.

It's really about understanding who your best-fit customers are based on the value you can deliver to those customers and the business outcome you can help them achieve.

The importance of owning your community

In the next chapter we will talk about which social networks to be on. That said, if you added all the subscribers for Facebook, Twitter, Google+, LinkedIn, Pinterest, Instagram, Blogger and YouTube, you would end up with close to half the population of Earth. Ninety-eight per cent of all social networks are basically free to use. Granted, there is some overlap, but even a conservative estimate of users would still be more than 2 billion people no matter what!

If we focus on B2B sites then in the case of LinkedIn we are now in the situation that if you are not on LinkedIn then you don't exist.

Business to Business and Business to Consumer companies have to this point seen the battle to gain market share, competitive advantage and ultimately revenue and profit as an offline task. Companies at a macro (corporate) and micro (employee) level need to wake up and move the fight online. They need to build their own communities to drive their message and share; not in a controlling, corporate way, but using the commonalities of community we discussed earlier, adding value to your community members, being supportive and sharing.

As outlined above, companies need to find and create a community so they move from carrying their own torch, to having a community that carries it for them. They become the lord of the manor, with customers, employees and even better still a wider network working to their common good.

A great example of this in the B2C space is gambling companies. Gambling is a highly regulated industry so they cannot advertise and say 'come gamble with me and your life will be complete' as they may have in the past. They create communities using humour, asking questions and getting interaction. We know of people who don't gamble, but follow and interact with the gambling sites as it's fun. You might be thinking, why would I want to interact with people who are not customers? As marketers/social salespeople, the opportunity is to use social as a way to get new customers. Those people we know who interact with gambling sites might one day decide to gamble and who do you think they will turn to? Yes, the company with whom they have the best connection or affinity.

One of the key strengths of social selling is using social techniques to find new prospects to convert to customers. The community will find you connections, people that don't even know your product or service exists, and turn them into ToFu (Top of the Funnel) prospects. Community will also nurture those prospects as they undertake their research in the market MoFu (Middle of the Funnel). Strength of community should also allow prospects to approach you; we would call this 'inbound'.

A word of warning: it's understandable that you might not believe this and hope this social media stuff will go away. But just remember that your competitors will be reading this (we hope) and they may be building a network to pull customers and prospects away from you into their network and community. You don't just press a button and create a community. Like the lord of the manor you need to grow and nurture one.

Battle of the networks

The connected community means that your prospects, customers and competitors are all now online. Customers, B2B and B2C can go on-line and discuss (good or bad) your brand, products and services. Word-of-mouth marketing has always existed in the offline world, but the connected society has accelerated the speed and distance that good and bad news can travel.

Engaging prospects early and often in the decision cycle is now a prerequisite of modern business, and the battle for attention is fought through subject matter expertise and thought leadership in a non-promotional format. Conversion of that hard-earned attention into prospects and leads is a combination of science and art, one that few understand.

Done right, the result provides branding, awareness, thought leadership, reputation, demand generation and lead nurturing.

We salespeople have always been 'control freaks'. Twenty years ago I was selling into the healthcare market in the UK. The accounting software company I worked for had no customers in that area. We worked hard on selling the first deal and made sure the implementation went well. That customer (while most customers will always justify a decision) went out of their way to tell people how great we were. This helped us sell the second deal. We then created a healthcare user group, which was an environment for the customers to exchange ideas and best practice. They also fed back into product development. This user group helped to sell the third, fourth and fifth deal, and so on. We became market leaders and then controlled the narrative. A number of competitors looked at what we had created and must have said, 'I want some of that', and we often had them sniffing around. We gave them six months before they lost interest. Why? We would like to say it was our great selling techniques, but it was because of our strength of network. Twenty years on, those organizations are still using the products I sold. I was in a meeting recently where a salesperson discussed a plan to try to sell a prospect a new system and he said, 'It's really difficult to sell to them, they are very loyal and have a strong community and network'.

'Every organization, commercial or public sector, has some information or capabilities that are worth more sharing than keeping to itself', says Frank Buytendijk of Gartner. Speaking in 2015, he goes on to say that, 'by 2018, one out of three businesses will be monetizing their information' (Levy, 2015). We think that with the need to create content to support communities and networks this figure is low.

Move that notion offline: online and through an online community you have the ability to shift markets and take markets from competitors. If you are a small business you can, at very little cost, undertake David and Goliath situations. If you are a major corporation, if you are not proactively creating community, companies will steal your market share. Community is the new competitive advantage.

Many people reading this might be in a situation where your competitor has already embarked on a community-building project. This is fine. While you could employ a company that writes books on community, there is an action plan you can deploy right now, which we will cover in the rest of the book.

Community exists online and offline. It can be built with your customers and employees as well as your industry influencers.

FIGURE 1.1 Control that brands have on author

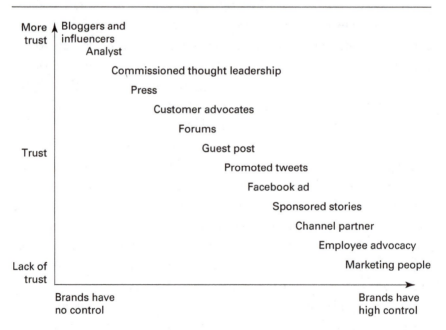

As you build the community you need to understand that people trust certain types of message and don't trust others.

In low socially mature organizations, it is seen as the norm that the employees are used to push out a corporate message. Organizations like 'employee advocacy' programmes as they can control the message and increase the noise out in the market. The view is that we should be 'doing' social and if we throw enough mud at the wall some of it will stick. Managers have often shown me reports where they are very proud as they have thrown more mud than their competitors. This is all well and good, but prospects and customers will say, 'Of course that employee will say that, they work there and are therefore biased'.

Corporations get control, but your prospects and customers won't trust the message.

As we move up the curve, organizations will engage in turning customers into references and references into advocates. Customer references are where organizations will say how great you are but do so in the confines of what you want to hear. This enables you to get your message out and we might trust it more than employees but we all know there is corporate control.

For many corporations moving up the curve is scary, as they lose control of the message. Moving to the position where our customers are more than just references, they are advocates, is where we lose control of the message, but the community finds it of a higher value. The fact that there may well be bad mixed with good can actually amplify the good. We are more likely to trust that message. If we trust that message, we will amplify and share it without our communities and tribes. Being open and supportive in your community gains you wider sharing and amplification.

The highest level of maturity is to find influencers to discuss and amplify your message. If you can get other 'lords of the manor' to positively discuss and share items about your brand then you will grow your community as they give you access to their communities. This is very scary for brands, as while you may gain a high level of trust, you have no control over what those influencers will say.

Further on in this chapter we discuss how to work with these 'tribe masters' and not do what I've seen, which is to try to use analogue methods. For example, in the past, brands have used 'Vice Presidents' because they were after all important in approaching influencers. But in the connected economy, the tribe masters have seen these people on social networks with little or no social profile, and have just laughed at their approach, in many cases going onto social networks to do so. These brands are then into a brand damage limitation exercise.

In Chapter 9 we show an organizational social maturity model, where we will discuss how employee and customer advocacy programmes can work as you move up the model.

Not too long ago DVDs ruled the world. For years, the DVD store Blockbuster seemed unbeatable. At its peak, the company operated 10,000 stores globally, and in 2002 had a market value of US $5 billion.

Many of us have seen the David and Goliath story of how Netflix swept Blockbuster away and became a must-have for 'teenagers'. Netflix seemed to have come out of nowhere for many of us (maybe living in the UK). But it actually started in 1997 as a start-up and built a distribution model that relied exclusively on mailing DVDs to customers through the low-cost US postal service. It was as convenient as a Blockbuster neighbourhood store but at a fraction of the price – and without the late fees that annoyed Blockbuster customers.

In 2007 Netflix started a streaming video service. This was a pretty visionary move for CEO Reed Hastings, as less than 50 per cent of US homes at that time had a broadband connection. Netflix disrupted the market by creating a new business model that pushed their major competitor into bankruptcy in 2011 and full shutdown by 2014.

Netflix have also created a community and tribe, where word-of-mouth recommendations are driving people to the channel and teenagers beg their parents to take subscriptions just so they can watch their favourite shows. Netflix is now moving into the area of original content (it has to, as content is king) to drive the next level of growth. It will affect television companies like BBC and ITV, as well as removing the need for postage, disrupting the third-party logistic companies.

Like the offline Coke and Pepsi wars of the past, with marketing and advertising moving online, so do the brands. While many B2C brands have led the way, many still work very much with analogue methods in the digital world.

In this online world there need to be new methods and best practice. Companies, big or small, must go online and form and build communities, using new strategies and techniques. Social karma requires corporations to think differently, to think about their customer, create a community and advocates, and maybe even work with competitors. For many people this is a scary thought, but help is at hand. There is a new type of person for whom this is second nature.

In the next section we will talk about the 'changemaker', somebody for whom community comes as second nature, where they probably sit in your organization, and how you can employ them to take your fight online.

Building your community

Twenty years ago, many salespeople will have had a 'little black book' of contacts or a Rolodex of business cards. Often jobs were given as a result of how big your contact group was. Then came sites like Ecademy and LinkedIn, and people moved their business card list online. But how many people do you know that use this to create a community? They tend to be 'one-dimensional' groups or lists of people.

Within your organization – and I doubt they will be currently in the boardroom – will be people for whom social is second nature. One of my salespeople admitted to me that his dog had 2,000 followers on Twitter. Martin (not his real name) was a sales guy we always went to as part of a social selling roll-out to try new ideas and techniques.

We would go to Martin and say, 'We are thinking of doing this'. He would try it and if it was a success, other salespeople would talk directly with him, learn from him and often slowly but surely the field adopted our ideas.

Social came naturally to Martin; he built his own blog and Twitter handle, he networked, shared, created content and built a community. He was the lord of the manor but also understood how to grow community and get his message out across other communities, thus allowing his own community to grow and thrive.

For sales organizations to grow, prosper and succeed in today's online world, they need a new person to be added to the team: the Social Community Manager (SCM).

Some of the sales leaders reading this will say this is Marketing's job and if you are working in a socially mature organization I understand the argument, but the only way your sales team will continually make their number, take competitive share from the competition and dominate your market is through you owning your community.

Are you really going to outsource success to another team, department or person rather than taking control of it yourself?

The SCM should not be mistaken for the community manager, who is often deployed in Marketing. Yes, the person needs to be comfortable in the world of social – they will create content – but that is where the similarity ends.

The SCM should be paid on the total quota for the sales team, since this binds them into the common goal of all the salespeople. They then help the salespeople build a community that allows you to 'sell'.

The mistake that most companies make in low socially mature organizations is to think that employee advocacy will work for the common good of the business. Sure it helps you blast corporate messages out there, but does it actually resonate with your market? When employees are following employees, are you just talking to yourself? Does anyone actually trust or believe anything an employee says? 'They would say that', after all.

When I first started out on social media I used to work with a guy in PR who had 1,000-plus followers on Twitter. A thousand followers is a 'platform' where you can start to form your own community. But when I did an analysis of his followers, I realized it was 'just' colleagues and the 'usual' PR agencies. Great 'business as usual' stuff, but it wasn't a community, there was little inter-sharing, and little crossover with other communities, so little chance of growth. Nice network, but little community.

Also, don't forget that salespeople come and go. In the connected society, social sellers will become the sought-after salespeople. Recruitment for salespeople with Klout scores of 50 and above will become the norm. On the basis that you have a wonderful culture and great products, you will lose people and their communities. This is why you need somebody to create community at a macro level, as well as help salespeople create community in their territories or at a micro level.

In the introduction we introduced the term 'Changemaker'. The SCM is a changemaker. A social selling project will require change, and while this needs to be sponsored at sales leader level, social selling requires this changemaker to drive it through the organization.

Let's stop a moment. If you are wearing a watch, take it off for me and put it on your other wrist. Notice how odd that feels; as you read this sentence you are thinking you want to switch it back to how you always have it. A number of you will have already moved it back by now. That is what we mean by change management. Digital and social require a new way of working and somebody needs to work with sales teams to help create that.

For the SCM to gain and maintain the respect of the other salespeople, they must sit within that team. We salespeople respect 'our own', people that have been at the 'coal face' and have been a 'bag-carrying salesperson'.

The SCM needs to be customer facing. To build a community they need to understand your customer, the business issues they are facing, and the competition. Customer meetings can soon be turned into blogs. How better to show the world you understand the issues they face than by sharing it in a blog?

Or better still the SCM should be looking to focus on what your customers will be doing in the future. Raise the game and offer to your customers real thought leadership, a direction in which you can lead. See the mountain top and lead your prospects there.

Regardless of whether you are a B2B company or you are targeting fly-fishing fans, people who love river cruises, or those who are Marvel comic fans, to build your community (and we talk about this in more detail in the following chapters) invite them to your site. Offer content that is specifically designed to fill their industry-specific needs. Hopefully they will start coming back for more.

We always suggest that the SCMs we work with go to a customer meeting, for example a meeting with the CFO (Chief Financial Officer) of a media company where they explain their top three business issues. You can come away from that meeting and type up those notes and add them to the CRM (customer relationship management) system.

In addition, you can take those notes, strip out any connection with that business or where they came from and post a blog: your point of view (POV) on the top three things impacting media companies right now. Don't mention your company or its services, but that article will flow out through your community. It will be picked up by other leaders in that market and this will help you grow contacts and enhance your standing. At some point in the future it may even create inbound.

In the B2B enterprise space that we tend to work in, the average salesperson we deal with has difficulty enough in understanding social. (The next chapter on personal branding should help you get started.) They have difficulty with the idea of being shared and are afraid they may make a fool of themselves. Some would even call them 'social phobics'. Anything about social sees them freeze and their eyes glaze over. If you are one of these people, even if you are a sales leader, then this book is a manual to help.

But we see in our training that often sales leaders and sales professionals say they 'get it', when in fact they don't. This is the area that is most dangerous to organizations. People who dabble in social and have not built community, even if they are seen as leaders in social, are not going to drive your business forward. They might talk a good story but if they could have, they would have. Again, just because somebody has a fancy job title, they too, if they haven't already created community, will carry on having just the fancy job title.

As we discussed in the introduction, the changemaker will probably have been you 10 years ago and they may be on track to be the next sales leader. You must now give them the delegated authority to provide the leadership and the vision to take the next step and jump into social.

The SCM will be the helmsperson to drive the vision, moving the organization through the various social maturity steps while also providing coaching and tutoring. In the social selling projects we have been involved in, we have found that one-to-one coaching is the only way to get people who say they 'get it' to admit they don't, and help them to understand and get on board with the project. In our experience, it is often these people who, once they get over the initial reluctance, see the political wind is changing and help you and the SCM in rolling out success.

TABLE 1.1 Attributes of a Social Community Manager (SCM) in the digital age

Sales	SCM
Content curation for salesperson's niche	Content curation across sales team as a whole
Building community within accounts	Building community and going to market
Still out in front of customers	Customer facing
Building influence within niche and accounts	Commercially aware
	Changemaker within sales team
	Makes it more likely people will buy from sales

Once an SCM is in place that person will need to drive the social selling project. Before they do that there needs to be a clear plan and elements in place.

The organization needs to understand who their customer is. Yeah, I know we have sold to them for years and years, but do we really know them?

Customer personas need to be developed and documented. A persona is the DNA of the person you are targeting, what makes them 'tick'. There may be many different personas in the same department.

For example, in the finance department there is the Finance Director or Chief Finance Officer (CFO), Financial Accountant, Management Accountant and Systems Accountant. Each has different wants, needs and personal wins. In any sales situation you may well be selling to multiple people and will therefore have different personas.

Finance people are often seen as continuous learners and like to be seen in organizations as the go-to for the latest information. They tend to see work as taking place during daytime boundaries. For example, if you send them a LinkedIn connection request at 8 pm, they won't accept it until the next working day. Finance departments tend to be fact based, and perhaps less inclined towards infographics than a table of figures.

Marketing directors tend to see themselves as the 'new' society guardians; they will be connected at all times. Send them a LinkedIn request at 8 pm and they will accept it then, as they will still be online. There is a clear blurring of online and offline boundaries. Marketing directors tend to love infographics, while finance directors, who tend to want more detailed facts, do not.

What community is not

Before we summarize the chapter, it is worth capturing what community is not. First and foremost, community is not measured in the number of followers you have. We are aware of people with 400 followers who, because of their niche, have been able to build a community. That is, people working for a common goal, sharing ideas and information, without expectation of financial gain. It is often a synergistic relationship, working for the common good. Salespeople need to do this within their territory and the SCM needs to do this to get the coverage across the teams to go to market.

As mentioned above, community has a true value when connections – people, business and things – are not static followers but when they all start to interact with each other. The number of connections can, at low cost, create an effect that exponentially multiplies value. Give and take provides an active and dynamic network of connections. The SCM acts as a guiding light in the middle of the organization, acting as the main influencer in a tightly woven fabric, a 'mesh' of connects.

This book is not about the pros and cons of Klout; we will leave that for others to comment on. While Klout isn't really a measure for low socially mature organizations, in organizations with middle-ranking social maturity it can provide a measure of social community. Why? People make the mistake of thinking that LinkedIn = social selling, and it does not. LinkedIn is only 30 per cent of your social graph.

For example, you may be calling upon somebody who is the sister-in-law of somebody you know. You might not get that information from LinkedIn, as often family relationships are not captured there, while on Facebook they would be. For somebody to be truly social and to build a community they need to do this across multiple platforms. We turn to our social leader the SCM to drive this.

Summary

In this chapter we took you through why community is so important in the digital and social age. Tribes and community come naturally to humans, and brands must grasp community as a way to sell and control their market online. Any organization has competitors and you need to treat community as your competitive advantage; it should not be seen as some sort of fluffy concept.

To build community you need to embrace today's changemakers, the SCMs, to drive that change. They are new leaders for the digital age; they might not be senior in your organization, but they will stand out as leaders in the world of Social and Digital.

Bonus material

The following bonus supporting resources are available at **www. koganpage.com/socialselling** (please scroll to the bottom of the web page and complete the form to access these).

- How community can drive innovation and Research and Development (R&D).
- Creating and working with Persona Selling.

Your identity within social networks

02

In the previous chapter we looked at how community and tribes were central to us in the offline world and how key they are to us in the online world.

In this chapter, we're going to be looking at our own identity within the constellation of social networks that are available to us. In the last chapter we learnt about the importance of community, and being able to take a leadership position within that community. Now we need to start putting the things in place to achieve that. We will also look at personal branding and how you can set yourself up on a social network.

Throughout this book we're keen to impress upon you the importance of focusing on social networks and not spreading yourself too thinly; you have to go where your customers are. As of the time of writing, the best B2B platforms are in our opinion LinkedIn and Twitter. This chapter will explain how to set up profiles on these platforms. Importantly, we look at how to frame and present our identity on both in a way that is both helpful to us, ultimately creating a leadership position within the community, as well as being appealing to customers.

Recently, I put out a request on LinkedIn to interview people that were not just using social selling but could quote a real Return on Investment (ROI). I was also interested in people that were using social not just for demand generation but through the whole of the sales process. A number of people made contact with me who saw social as key for pipeline creation/demand generation, but also for nurturing leads through the pipeline.

The number one piece of advice I received was to know your target markets, listen, engage and interact with them. When you build trust with people, they will also open their networks to you. In addition, there was that old adage that salespeople need to be proactive. Also, there is a 'hippy' sales fraternity who see Social as a way of being nice and not as a sales tool we can use to create business, so don't forget to ask for the sale. I'm not saying here that you have to be aggressive, as asking for the business should just 'flow'.

Is there a programmatic approach?

Twitter is for connecting; look for the signals, then switch to DM (direct mail), e-mail or telephone. Once the person is connected, you can link to them on LinkedIn to stay in touch and nurture. You also get access to their networks.

We will now go through what you need to do to set up a LinkedIn profile. There are many books on personal branding and this is not a step-by-step process, but an overall vision of what a good LinkedIn profile and Twitter account should look like.

LinkedIn

LinkedIn have managed to get to a position where if you're a professional in any industry (as buyer or seller), it's perceived that you have to be on LinkedIn. It's almost like the 2016 equivalent of how it felt to have a business card in the 1990s – you didn't really have a job unless you had a business card with your job title on it. Today you don't 'exist' unless you have a LinkedIn profile.

But it's not all about setting up a profile; LinkedIn can be used as your address book (people will always update their details so the addresses are never out of date) and it can also be used as a lead nurture tool.

Getting started

If you unpick LinkedIn to the point where it is just a directory (albeit an international, universal one), your LinkedIn profile is your listing in that directory. It is an advert for you that anybody in the world can see and it's visible 24 hours a day, 365 days a year.

Your profile will be looked at by two audiences, which are:

- People who have come to look at it because some signal from elsewhere has pointed them at it. For example, a friend or colleague may have recommended you and they've come to find you; you've asked to link to them and they want to know who you are; you've posted some content on LinkedIn or elsewhere and they want to know more about you.

- People who have come to look at it because they have found you in some search. Those are two fundamentally different things – either someone is looking for more information (they're coming in warm), or they have no idea who you are at all (they're coming in cold).

Fundamentally, your listing is an advert, and like any advert it has to be engineered to get the viewer to take action. At a minimum you want them to follow you. At a maximum you want to be so compelling they contact you and ask to set up a meeting.

This advert is your personal brand to the world. When people look at your profile they have a first impression of who you are. In the past a first impression would have been made when you were introduced; now because of the internet anybody can search for you and get that first impression. Wouldn't it be great if that first impression created a next action that got you an enquiry about your business or service, thus reducing the amount of proactive prospecting you need to do?

One of the underlying themes of this book is that social sellers have to be much better at marketing than traditional sellers. The traditional salesperson tends to rely on marketing to do a lot of the market-softening aspects of marketing for them (for example, branding, and advertising). In social selling, the market-softening aspects have to be done as part of the general sales process. Specifically in this case, your LinkedIn profile has to be an advert.

Your advert has to have the following aspects:

- a well-developed position;
- well-crafted, customer-centric (interesting to a customer rather than a recruiter) messaging around that position;
- very little in the way of stuff the customer doesn't care about;
- a clear call to action.

Setting yourself up on LinkedIn

You should have a colour photo; this is a professional network and people are taking away a first impression of you from this profile. You can put up that photo of you in a bar in Spain, but I wouldn't recommend it. People might not see you as relaxed and social as you'd hope; they might just decide that you spend your life in a bar. Is that the impression you want to give?

You should show your full name, but in addition to this, any 'known as' names. For example, my birth name is Timothy, but I'm known as Tim. See also Michael and Mike, Robert and Rob or Bob, for example. This allows people to find you if they search by any version of your name, eg Tim Hughes, rather than Timothy Hughes.

Your LinkedIn profile is an advert for you. It is up 24 hours a day and 365 days a year. As we discussed earlier, the world has changed and buyers are now going online and researching what they want to buy. They are highly informed. Most buyers, when they go online, are doing so in 'salesperson avoidance mode'. To that end, if you look like a salesman then they will avoid you.

The key to this is the 'buyer-centric' profile. That is, a profile which appeals to a buyer in research mode. If your LinkedIn profile is older it is probably laid out as a CV so you can be found by headhunters and get your next job. This again is old fashioned.

To be 'buyer-centric' you have to appeal to the buyer if they come across you. You need to be intriguing, educational, supportive, helpful and ultimately encourage the buyer to take a next action, which is to contact you.

For example, if you sell filing cabinets, a traditional profile will show how many times you have made quota. As a buyer, I might think you are more willing to win the sale and make your quota than to get me the product that meets my needs.

The alternative might be to put on your profile a blog article (written by you) called 'Top 10 things to think about when buying filing cabinets'. This helps and educates. It might be important to understand the differences between a foolscap size versus A4. The fact that I then make the right buying decision could lead me to recommend and become an advocate for you, bringing you more sales.

Don't forget your contact details at the bottom of that article, but more on calls to action (CTAs) later.

People are also making decisions on what people are like based on their profiles. If, like me, you research people before you meet them, you will make a judgment just by looking at their profile as to how well a meeting will go and whether you even want to do business with that company. We often decide before a meeting how we think that meeting will go based on what a person's LinkedIn profile looks like.

If you sell a product or service that is expensive or will be used by an organization for a long time, buyers are looking for long-term relationships, and will be seeking thought leaders and people they can partner with, not quota crushers.

We will keep coming back to being buyer-centric.

If you Google yourself, it is your name and job title that is visible and you want a buyer to take a next action and click on you.

The job title needs to be buyer-centric. It is understandable you are very proud to have built up your career over time to become a Master Principal Consultant, and that is probably your internal grade. But for the buyer it's most probably meaningless and does not sound like it can help them.

To be buyer-centric you need to think about your output – what is the business impact you make with customers? Do you make their customer services more efficient? Reduce inventory? How is it that you help them? What is it you think you can teach them? It usually takes time (and multiple iterations) to come up with something you feel comfortable with.

The next section is the summary. The summary also needs to be buyer-centric if you have got a prospect this far; it needs to be compelling and educational. What business issues have you solved, customers you have helped? How can you help prospective customers in the future? Have a 'call to action (CTA)' where somebody can make contact with you.

The section should be 'output' based and also contain 'keywords' that prospective customers might use to search for your product or services. Avoid buzzwords and internal jargon. Often in the B2B community we can be fixated on our own terminology, not considering that the customer has no idea what we are talking about.

You should also upload some video/multimedia content below the summary. Some people put company videos, which is a 'cop out'. Corporate videos show your employer how committed you are, but they can make you look very 'corporate suit'. You are supposed to be helping somebody to buy, not just replicate your employer's website.

You can create your own video content cheaply and easily. Get a colleague to interview you, just using your smartphone, and upload that. It does not need to be more than five minutes.

We also recommend you have a background photo or picture as this brightens up the profile. In my case I use a photo I took of the sun rising. Key thing is not to be 'one dimensional' but to bring the profile alive.

How to find the keywords to use

Go to Google.com (make sure you're signed out of Gmail and Google) and start entering words that you think people might use to find you, or your products and services. Google will auto-populate suggestions for searches. These suggestions are top searches performed on Google by other people. This should help you get a feeling for the keywords you need to 'bury' or 'build around' in your summary.

Completing job roles on LinkedIn

It may come as a surprise to some readers but unlike five years ago where your LinkedIn profile was a copy of your CV, as you were using it to get your next job, now it is being used by you to inform, teach and support your prospective customers.

In my LinkedIn profile, I provide key facts (with keywords) and also back this up with recommendations. Recommendations are key, especially from customers or third parties you have worked with, to demonstrate this isn't just something you have thought up and put out on spec.

Again, the way you describe your job should be output based. What is it in your role that you do to support customers?

Volunteer experience and causes

We certainly recommend that you itemize any voluntary work or charity work, as this shows the reader that you are a rounded and worldly person. I itemize all the sponsored cycle rides I've been on; life isn't all about me.

Education

Itemize significant education you have achieved; in my case I mention my university qualification. This does not mean you need to mention every single swimming and cycling certificate. If you have achieved any training or qualifications as part of your role, such as sales or marketing training, first aid, languages etc, then they are worth mentioning.

Organizations

If you are part of any organizations outside of work then it would be worth mentioning them, such as involvement with your children's school, charitable or professional bodies, especially if they are useful for your work.

Skills and recommendations

Recommendations are different from skills on a LinkedIn page. Skills are used by recruiters to search for the people they want for a role. If you want recruiters to find you then it is worth spending some time working on which of these are appropriate for you.

In addition, it is worth you thinking about what it is that people around you, your family and friends, would also think about you – if you are loyal or trustworthy etc. Again, you don't have to be 'corporate suit' and you can add and change these around to suit your own personality. I'm not saying you do, but I know people who want it to be known that a key skill for them is 'chocolate' or 'indie rock'.

Positioning and messaging

For a marketer, positioning is about having a clear focus as to who your customer is and what they want. Your job when developing a position is to get to a point where a human being understands your position and then wants to engage further. That necessitates someone seeing your position, which is what advertising is. Seeing as LinkedIn profiles are adverts, it follows that the job of a LinkedIn profile/advert is to get your position across.

Messaging is the execution of positioning. Positioning is the part you understand as a business – 'we want to sell hosted telephony systems to this sort of company'. Messaging is how you present the position. If you're a luxury brand advertising in a luxury magazine (eg Vogue), your messaging will be highly visual. On LinkedIn, our messaging has to be the written word.

The most important thing about a position is that it has to be focused. What kills marketing more than anything (and by extension any commercial proposition depending on that marketing) is being too broad. If you sell hosted telecoms, a poor position would be to say that you can sell that to anyone. It's much better to have focus and say that you're 'going to sell to companies in or around London, in the legal sector, with turnover of £x'. The reason for this is that it's easier to craft messages around a focused position. Consider 'We sell hosted telecom systems', versus 'As an IT manager for a London-based mid-sized law firm, we understand the importance of one-click dialling to you, that's why we've crafted this special solution that does speed dialling.'

That said, it's likely you don't have a free hand in this market position as the business likely already has one. Your job as a social salesperson is to fully understand the business's market position, and then craft a good message around it.

Buyer persona

Crafting a message is dependent on having well-defined personas. A persona is an expression, usually a written expression, of a sample customer. They are usually quite detailed and talk about the person in professional and personal terms. Often there are amalgams of a small set of customers the company already has who are strategically important. If your marketing team isn't particularly good, they may not have developed personas. As a salesperson doing 'smarketing' or, as it's sometimes called, 'smales' (sales and marketing together), you will need personas to craft your messaging.

A persona is the DNA of the person you need to target. Not just a job title, but the elements that make them up. Are they professional? What networks do they hang out in? What is the structure of their life? Are they visually or factually orientated?

By looking at human, emotional and rational factors, propositions can be based on two-dimensional rational and emotional reason to believe. In many cases people also layer on the purpose the company fulfils on a human or societal level.

For example, human resources directors tend to have blurred boundaries around work and an InMail sent at 8 pm might get a response right away. They also tend to be more visual so an infographic might be deployed. On the other hand a finance director will tend to work at set times and be more factual. They generally prefer facts rather than an infographic.

Developing personas is outside of the scope of this book, but we will offer some pointers in case your marketing team don't have them and can't be cajoled in to developing them for you. Essentially, it's an imaginary person that you want to talk to. Write down who they are, what they do, what their pains are, what their motivations are, and how they need to be conveyed from being a prospect to a customer. You may have multiple personas. The critical aspect of this is that any messaging piece that you put together must be targeted to at least one of those personas. Effectively, you are writing for that person.

The purpose of doing this is that it carries the focus of the position through to the message, and by definition you'll only end up talking to people with whom the position resonates. It fundamentally makes it easier to put together messaging. Psychologically we are all very good at talking to one person and developing a relationship – we all intuitively understand how to do that. The converse of this – talking to a group of people in the hope that some of them will come over to our way of thinking – is much harder and hugely counterintuitive.

The most common mistake that people make with LinkedIn is to talk about themselves in their profile. That's fine if LinkedIn is a directory, but we're trying to use our profile like an advert. Presenting a market position through messaging that is seller-centric is the most basic marketing mistake that you can make.

Ironically, as a salesperson you already know this. You know that when talking to a customer you have to above all else listen to what they are telling you about themselves and their problems. Listen to who they are, what their struggles are, and what the impact of that pain is. Then develop with them a vision of what a solution might be and flesh out that solution. That approach works because it makes the customer feel understood and comfortable – it moves you both into a joint partnership position of trying to reach a common goal, rather than you as the salesperson imposing a solution on them.

And so it needs to be like this with your positioning.

Is this a good message for a customer?

- *'Twenty years' experience selling telephony solutions.'*
  No – that's a good message for an employer. If I was a sales manager of a company that sold hosted telephony solutions and wanted to hire someone for my team – that's a roughly good enough message. But the customer – someone looking to buy a hosted telephone solution – frankly could not care less about this messaging.

- *'Hosted telephony can be a great way to increase the reliability of your phone system.'*
  OK, so now we have something that's not good for an employer, but is better for a customer. This underlines the importance of focus when it comes to positioning – is your profile for an employer or a customer? You can't have both – you have to have focus. In this case, we've focused on the customer.

With your developed market position and personas you can now go and craft your message within the summary box.

You may well be thinking 'easier said than done'. Indeed, it will take some practice, some iterations, and 'socializing' it with friends and colleagues. ('Socializing' in this context means circulating it, asking for feedback, and then taking that feedback on board.) The important thing is to get something written, get some input, and then tweak. The only mistakes that you can make are talking too much about yourself, and not having focus.

Calls to action

Every advert needs a call to action (CTA). Whatever the advertising medium, it costs time and money to get people to look at an advert. People viewing adverts have to be actively encouraged to take an action that you want, which is why marketers insist on having a clear CTA on adverts.

Some people viewing your advert will do nothing, because it's not of interest to them. However, to some people what you're offering (ie your 'position') will be of interest. The worst possible outcome is someone sees your advert, is interested, but then doesn't understand what the next steps are. An obvious analogy is of a fish wriggling off the hook as you're trying to land it.

Of course, what your CTA is may not be clear. We know people who put their mobile number on their profile and ask people to call them. We know others that want users driven to their Twitter account, or some other webpage. Think of the customer journey here; if somebody has taken the time and trouble to research you so far on the web, will they pick up the phone to you? It might be better to offer them a 'web' solution, getting them to connect with you or driving them to your blog for example.

Whatever your CTA is, it has to be crafted into your summary section. We've gone through quite a lot of detail on the problems with CTAs really just to focus your mind on the fact you have to do something which is good enough. When you've done your summary section, and you're socializing it around your friends and colleagues, make sure that your CTA is clear, and that you test it during that socialization.

The worst possible way of using LinkedIn

Most users' frustration with LinkedIn is that people use it as a channel for interruption marketing. It's very likely that you have experienced this.

The approach goes as follows. LinkedIn doesn't want people sending InMails (their equivalent of e-mails) in great numbers, and hence make them in relative terms extremely expensive. So instead salespeople use the search function, and fill out the 'We've done business together' connection form. More socially open people on LinkedIn will accept any invitation. As soon as that invitation is accepted that person becomes a first-level connection and you instantly get back a message like this:

FIGURE 2.1 The worst possible way of using LinkedIn!

Dear Matt!

Our companies work in closely related fields and that's why I've contacted you. I noticed that you work for Influencer Insights

There is an opportunity to find mutual point of interest for both of us. Our main business is to provide software engineers to customers' needs. We have more than 200 developers and narrowly specialize in PHP, .Net, Java and iOS, Android and Windows Phone. The average price rate for a middle developer is 25 Euro per hour and 30 Euro for a senior developer. We can help your team to handle your software technology needs and assist in software development.

I'll be in your area on October 5th–9th and will be able to meet you to discuss some possible projects.

I would appreciate your feedback.

We can all recognize that as spam. I would struggle to care less about this offer, this person, or their business.

Don't do that.

Twitter

As of the time of writing in 2016, we believe social salespeople should be on both LinkedIn and Twitter. The objective of this chapter is to get your identity in these platforms sorted out. As we go through into other chapters, the objectives will be to teach you how to use both of these to build up your community, as introduced in Chapter 1.

As we discussed, LinkedIn primarily looks to model real-world connections, and does this through a directory metaphor. It assumes that people have already met, and just want a digital alternative to meeting in real life.

Twitter, on the other hand, is geared towards letting people who don't know each other yet form relationships based on shared ideas and goals. What this means from a social selling perspective is that there are people out there ideating solutions to complex problems, whom you can actually get at. Thus, you will find it significantly easier to find and engage with potential (not yet spoken to) customers on Twitter compared to LinkedIn.

The behaviour that you are looking for on Twitter is that as a salesperson you put something interesting out into the network, and that your actions will stimulate a user into doing something.

Twitter ROI

I'm aware of people that have spent £20,000 per annum on advertising for just a few hundred pounds worth of income. A connection of mine started to use Twitter, and for no expenditure other than his time, he got over £2,000 of business in two weeks. He now averages £500 a month via Twitter.

How to be social – sharing ideas

With all social networks, the key is in the first word 'social'; the idea is not to put out endless updates but to get engagement and comment.

The value of the comments (or better still questions) is that they are valuable in and of themselves, and because they are directly attributable to the author, readers tend to attribute value and worth to the author. This makes it very easy to build thought leadership positions.

The reason we are talking about this is that your identity on Twitter is far more defined by your behaviour and how you present yourself than on LinkedIn. LinkedIn is a lot more sanitized and 'advert-like', whereas Twitter is considerably more 'human'. Plus, there is an advantage to positioning yourself as a 'purveyor of new ideas', compared to someone who just circulates other people's ideas.

That said, what we didn't talk about in the section on LinkedIn was the idea of news. Although at its core LinkedIn is a directory, it has a way of allowing a member to post news articles that might be of interest to that member's network. If you go to the home page in LinkedIn and you're logged in, you'll see posts from people that you have connected with, or that you follow. (This idea is called content curation, and we'll talk about this in much more detail in Chapter 8 on technology.)

Your Twitter profile

Users are attracted to other people on Twitter based on what that person posts, rather than who they are. However, your Twitter profile is important as often what will happen is that people will look at your profile before deciding whether to follow you or not. As we'll see in Chapter 5, it's important to build up your followers, and your profile will either help or hinder that process.

Your profile should contain a picture, a short piece of biographical information about yourself, a link to a website, and a location. Your profile should be about you as a person, not about the business, and as a result the picture should be of you and not the business. A good number of people make the mistake of branding their Twitter account for the business and not them as an individual. The whole point of having a social profile is to allow potential buyers to find you and then hopefully engage. People form an opinion of you from your Twitter and LinkedIn profiles and if you have a photo of a corporate then they will think you are just that, a corporate.

The location is important, as although the network is global, you need to focus your efforts on where your customers are. For example, hosted telephony may be a globally applicable business, but your ultimate goal is to get meetings, and you need to be able to get to them. Part of this focus is being clear in your location information as to where you are. Our further advice on this would be to make this unambiguous. (In the UK, for example, there is a Sudbury in West London and one in Suffolk, so 'Sudbury, West London' or 'Sudbury, Suffolk' is better on a profile.) Further, putting your country on is also a good idea to make it very clear to potential followers where you are – for example, 'Sudbury, Suffolk, UK'.

Your bio should describe succinctly your leadership role in your new community, and the value that you intend to bring to people interested in that community. Of course, it should be aligned with your marketing position and attendant messaging. For example: 'Helping people get the best from hosted telephony solutions'.

In the bio, you can reference other Twitter handles, but any web links that you put in there will not be clickable. However, you need to consider your CTA on your profile. If someone is looking at your profile, you want them to follow you immediately, rather than get distracted and go off following something else. However, it's beneficial to use other handles to build brand and authority – for example, 'Helping people get the best from hosted telephony solutions. Co-founder of @MyHostedTelephonySolutions – ideas around hosted telephony' helps build authority, albeit at the expense of reducing the number of people who action your desired CTA of following your account.

Finally there is the web link. This one web link will be clickable, but again remember that it will affect the CTA. On a company Twitter profile this should be the company website. On a personal account, the objective is less clear. You have to consider the action you want. Just dumping a user at the home page of the website likely doesn't do anything particularly helpful – the user will consider the website, but seeing as most company websites do not have a clear CTA on that page you'll end up wasting the click. It likely makes more sense to send them to your LinkedIn profile. The LinkedIn profile will re-inforce your position, and also has a clear-ish CTA objective in getting a 'follow' over on that side.

Structure of a Twitter profile

With Twitter the fundamentals are the same as with a LinkedIn profile; it needs to be buyer-centric. If a buyer looks at your Twitter profile, what is it that will make them want to follow you or even make contact with you?

You need a photo, as above; this is about your personal brand. First impressions count. I recommend getting a professional shot done. You should also use the same photo across all your professional networks – it's a personal brand after all.

Some corporate organizations make recommendations as to what your profile should say and I would follow them. That said, you don't want to look like a corporate suit; be original, funny even. But be professional. Say a little bit about yourself. Have a website people can go to for more information. The corporate website is fine, but this is also a great opportunity to drive traffic to your blog. You need to decide if you want to have one account for everything you do, or a separate account specifically directed to your company.

In the United States it is the law that if you have gained followers during work time, then they belong to your employer. For example, if you built up a large following and went to a competitor, that following that your previous employer had 'paid' to set up could then be used against them. In the United States there have been situations where the employee has been asked to hand the Twitter profile back. While this is not currently the law in the UK there have been high-profile cases where journalists for the BBC left to go to a competitor channel, and the BBC asked for the Twitter profile back. Of course, there was a mass unfollowing, as the people followed the journalist and not the BBC.

Some organizations suggest you need to add a disclaimer such as 'the views given here are my own and not representative of the business' into your avatar, but while this is standard policy, thinking has moved on. If it is a company account you speak for the company regardless of what is in your avatar. There have been some suggestions that employees start using a hashtag so that the reader can see the tweet is from or represents an employee view and not that of the organization. This often happens when organizations are at a low level of social maturity, and they are trying to regain control of social media. Corporations need to understand that the genie is out of the bottle with Social and they cannot control the flow of information.

IBM's social selling programme recommends that people should have one profile, so the follower gets a more 'rounded' view. A cynic might say that the IBM messaging might end up being more subliminal, rather than 'buy IBM', which I guess is what IBM want.

I split my Twitter accounts up, and constantly remind whomever I work for that the accounts belong to me. They are not another channel to pump out 'corporate' content.

The key thing is to be interesting and educational, and I think my accounts are educational.

I will also tweet competitor articles. My view is that social media in many cases is a ToFu (Top of the Funnel) or Middle of the Funnel (MoFu) activity and if it helps to educate the buyer then that is great. My role is to support the community or to get us on the short list. Who wins the deal, and how, is not my concern; that is down to the salespeople – good old sales skills.

With my Twitter profile, my name is straightforward, and for my work account I would add my company name into the title so it is clear whom I work for. This isn't about selling by 'stealth' or not being honest about who we are.

There is a short description, in which I try to show an element of a sense of humour, where I am based, and a call to action website, which in this case is my blog.

Avoid putting your corporate website on here if you can as it tends to be too broad.

Research shows that tweets with photos tend to get around 50 per cent more engagement than those without. It is not for this book to go in depth into how you craft a tweet, using hashtags etc.

LinkedIn and Twitter can be used to find people that you would like to speak to, speak to them online, move that conversation offline and then form an ongoing relationship with them.

Twitter as a social network can allow you to follow and be followed by people you don't know, whereas with LinkedIn you will probably know the person in some way. The key is to use both of these networks to complement each other and build your community.

The news feeds provide a way of offering content that your followers or future followers will find interesting and perhaps educational; better still they will want to engage with you.

Send a tweet

Have you managed to get your Twitter account set up? Why not send a tweet to us at @timothy_hughes and @mbrit? If you are feeling brave, send us a selfie of you and the book.

Summary

Changemakers are out there, building teams and looking to solve problems for their companies. To solve problems, look for new solutions – people are doing this by going online. While the obvious place to start would be a search engine, they are also using social networks to solve those problems. If you are in Business to Business (B2B) enterprise sales, having a personal brand is as important as having a mobile (cell). You don't exist without it. Personal branding is just level one; we now explain what you need to do to use social networks to help you over-achieve your quota.

Talking to strangers

03

'Networking in real life' example

One of the first things our parents or guardians tell us from an early age, apart from not to be late, is to never talk with strangers. Maybe that is why so many people find social media difficult; it goes against the parental messages that hide in our heads.

There is a video that does the rounds on social media every six months where somebody goes up to strangers in the street and starts following them. When challenged, the person says, 'I'm just being a follower'. The video also has a person going up to strangers and saying, 'Can I be your friend?'

Why am I pointing out the absurdity of social media in a social media book?

As children and as adults, talking to strangers is something we are taught is rude, and is certainly something introverts will avoid at all costs.

Networking is a term that has been used over recent years as the socially accepted way of saying, go into a room and talk to a bunch of people you have never met; strangers. Often we can break down people into introverts and extroverts. The introverts generally won't want to talk with strangers, whereas the extroverts usually will. But is there a way we can talk with strangers that will help us? I'm sure we can remember right back to our childhood when we first started school and we needed to talk to children we didn't know, but they soon became our friends. For some of us, they become friends for the rest of our lives.

In the world of sales, when we go for a first meeting with a client, we quickly need to create a connection between people as prospective customers and ourselves. That connection can be made from rapport, trust, mutual understanding and respect, and that all has to be built or created in a matter of minutes. Many of us recognize this in the offline world. Now we can (and have) to do this in the online world, as this is where our buyers in the connected economy are. Yes, our skills come into good use when we have face-to-face meetings, but we need to use social media to help us get those meetings.

As we have talked about in the previous chapters, this book is about helping you and short-cutting the demand generation process. You need to build a community so you are already recognized as a thought leader and a 'go to' for knowledge in your specialist subject or niche. This gives you the credentials so that people might seek you out. In the online world, as you start to contact and interact with people they will want to make sure you are not a spammer, which is why you need a decent social profile as covered in the last chapter. Building your online profile and community means you need to talk with many strangers; these people may be prospects, competitors and influencers already. We discuss in the first chapter the importance of people and brands in building a community and owning that community. To build that community we need to talk to a lot of strangers.

In the sales environment we will meet many different types of people: decision makers, influencers (internal and external), user decision makers and often, in the modern world, changemakers. As part of the selling process we need to 'meet' these people (offline and online) and work out if they are supporters that will enable us to make that sale. Owning the community where these people need to work and thrive will help us, but we need to talk (and interact) with these strangers and build long-term relationships with them. (We want our customers to become references and advocates as it helps us sell more. Plus, people move from company to company and we want them to take us with them in their new role.)

We have just received an invite to a networking party, so what do we do? We might take a friend, as that would ease the embarrassment of talking with strangers, but let's assume we go by ourselves. We might arrive, get a drink and either look around for a group that might 'look fun' or see somebody who is standing by him or herself and go up and talk to them.

If we take this example online, many people who I don't know contact me and follow or link to me. There's nothing wrong with that, and I have built many a long-term business relationship with people I have met online but in fact have never met in real life. Some I do, but there are still people I have known for many years yet have never met them in person.

What often happens is that people link with me and then send me a message by direct mail (DM) and tell me about how wonderful their product and service is. No context. For example, somebody approached me and told me how great their telephone system is. I'm sorry, but I'm not currently in the market for a telephone system and I'm unsure I will be in the future.

Let's go back to the networking event. How about I arrive, and before I get a drink I stand in the doorway and shout at the top of my voice, 'Hi, I'm Tim and I have this great telephone system!', then launch into my pitch... I'm sure this would silence the room for a few seconds and some people may stop to watch such a spectacle, but more likely to see my embarrassment. It is highly unlikely I will sell anything and even less likely I will be invited back! So if you don't do that in the offline world, why is it seen as OK behaviour in the online world?

Another mistake that people also make is that in that room of 100 people, they don't consider how many might actually be decision makers for telephone systems. Or will be in the future.

Listening to a presentation yesterday, it stated that 'everybody at that party will be useful for you.' I'm sorry, I don't buy that. If you go to a networking party of 100 people, it's clearly illogical to believe that more than 20 people will be useful to you. I'm sure being the acquaintance of all 100 would be great, as they may know somebody who knows somebody, but it's a physical impossibility to get round everybody at that event. So how do you find the 20 people who will be useful for you and your community?

Listening

Back to our networking event. Getting our drink we decide which person or group we will go and contact. Once we have made our introductions, we talk about who we are and what we do. If we have approached a group, rather than butting into a conversation, which would be deemed rude, we listen to what other people are saying. We might nod in agreement or encouragement. We might offer up our own examples. As time progresses we might ask open questions (how, what, where, why?). After a time we might provide our own commentary. Often we will judge this by the body language of the people in the group. When trust is built, then often there is a swapping of business cards. But how many times have you turned up to networking events and decided after a few minutes that the people you are talking to won't help you in your current goals and objectives?

How long do you give it before you make the decision to 'go and get another drink', which is the polite way of dropping those people and finding another group, one that will meet your common objectives? This is probably why speed dating became so popular, as it allows people to decide if there is a match within a couple of minutes. With the speed-dating concept the embarrassment of moving from person to person is taken away from you as you are forced to move on as part of the rules of the format.

There is a way you can talk to strangers and quickly qualify if they will be useful to you. In fact you can work that out before you contact them. You can do it on social media.

Before we dive into networking with hundreds of people on social media, let's talk about active listening, as it's different from hearing.

When we are in a conversation with somebody we often hear what they are saying, but I'm not sure we actually listen to what they say. Why? In any conversation, while somebody talks we are thinking about what we are going to say next – we may even be trying to work out a way to move the subject away from certain areas. Our mind is in another place.

That is the difference between hearing and listening. Listening is where we hear and maybe even note down what the person is saying.

I've often done this with customers where we have worked as a pair. There are two of you; one person asks the questions, then the next person, giving you both time to listen and hear what your customer or prospect is actually saying. Often you can use active question techniques and go back with, 'What does that mean to you?' or, 'What is that loss in $ value?'

There is a technique called 'active listening' which you can use with 'active questioning'. This is where you repeat back to the customer what they have said, not in a way that sounds like a trap but for example: 'This inventory loss sounds painful, if we could show you in a demonstration how we can reduce the shrinkage, do you think this would go some way to reduce the $ value of losses you are receiving right now?'

Such techniques can be used in the online world of social media to help you network and group your community.

In the world of Business to Business (B2B) sales we are recommending that you focus on initially Twitter and LinkedIn. Both of them have their advantages and both of them can be used in different 'modes' for both demand generation and through the sales process.

LinkedIn is ideal – and designed – for networking. Many people create their profiles, then meet somebody and receive a connection request. Many (most) people now research who they are going to meet by looking up their LinkedIn profile before the meeting. I will send LinkedIn connect requests before a meeting on the basis people can 'check out my shop window' and therefore make the meeting more productive.

LinkedIn, as described in the previous chapters, can also be used for searching for customers and prospects you don't know and approaching them.

Our usual approach is to use the active listening techniques discussed above when contacting somebody over social media and write: 'I noticed you were talking about XYZ – have you considered this?' This being some content that the contact will be interested in to drive the conversation forward.

By adding value and engaging (just like we would do in the offline world) we are able to quickly find the people we need to talk to and engage with them. For sellers this has major advantages as you are able to accelerate the selling process and get your products or services in front of the right people quicker.

When I first started selling 27 years ago, it was explained to me that when I met customers I would need to build rapport. 'How do I do this?' I asked. When you go to meetings with customers they will have photos on their walls. It might be fly-fishing, Formula One, or football – whatever it is that excites them. I was told to draw people into discussions about their passions, to listen and have a two-way dialogue, thus building rapport. Nothing has changed today, except that our offline world has moved online.

Twitter works well for our methodology, as you can follow your prospects and customers and listen to what they are saying at the macro (company) level or can also find and listen at the micro level to the individuals you are targeting. This enables you to listen to what is important to that company, and also get an understanding of the individuals in your territory. What is important to them? Even if they tweet about walking their dogs you know that their dogs are important. This is no different from walking into somebody's office and seeing photos of their dogs on the wall. Use it (and be authentic) as a way to build a conversation.

Your prospects and changemakers are out there leaving 'footprints' on social networks – you need to find them.

Social graph

The term 'social graph' was popularized at the Facebook F8 conference on May 24 2007, when it was used to explain how the newly introduced Facebook platform would take advantage of the relationships between individuals to offer a richer online experience. The definition has been expanded to refer to a social graph of all internet users. The social graph in the internet context is a graph that depicts the personal relations of internet users. It has been referred to as 'the global mapping of everybody and how they're related'.

While some people talk about social selling as just LinkedIn, it cannot be, as LinkedIn is only about 30 per cent of an individual's social graph. A person's social graph will cover all of the networks they belong to: LinkedIn, Facebook, Instagram, Google+, as well as e-mail contacts.

A friend of mine was researching a human resources (HR) director and couldn't find her on LinkedIn or Twitter, but did find her on Instagram, which is where she posted photos of her cats. He was able to build rapport and engagement with her through those cat photos, which led him to get a face-to-face meeting and then close the deal.

People often say to me, 'isn't this stalking?' No. If people are putting photos of their cats in an open network that everybody can see, then far from stalking, they will be flattered that you have taken the time to find them and I'm sure will like to talk about them.

A colleague of mine was calling upon a CEO of an organization. He did all the research and this CEO wasn't connected to any of his contacts on LinkedIn. What he didn't know was that this CEO was also the brother-in-law of a work colleague; that relationship didn't show up on LinkedIn but it would have on Facebook. People often say to me that Facebook is for friends and family and photos. Maybe, but don't forget that it is also part of your prospects' and customers' social graph. I'm not suggesting that you start walking all over Facebook selling your wares, but if you cannot see your contact's Facebook connections you are missing a serious part of their social graph.

A friend of mine, @Jon_Ferrara, is the CEO of the Social CRM product Nimble, a great tool that allows you to do research on somebody before a meeting. Jon set up a call with me a few years ago, which was where he was going to pitch his product to me. Some recent research showed that people were 40 per cent more likely to prefer going to the dentist than to receive a supplier pitch. I was sure Jon would be different, but I was knocked out by how different he was.

Jon is based in California. Usually what happens when I have a call with people on the US west coast (which is eight hours behind me in the UK) is a conversation about the weather and what time it is. Jon was different; he had done his research about me and his first question was, 'What's your favourite vinyl record?' We then spent the first 15 minutes of the call talking about vinyl and the bands we had seen. This level of rapport knocked me out and if we are ever in vinyl record shops we send each other photos.

This for me is such a great example of somebody that took the time to research me and found out that I collect vinyl records. In the first 15 minutes Jon built rapport (he also collects vinyl) and we got to know and trust each other better through our own respect of rock music. Jon 'nurtures' our relationship through that mutual interest by sending me photos of record shops or rare copies he has obtained. He and his product are then front of mind.

While social is a revolution it does not take away from what we have always done offline. We still need to talk with people and build relationships, but what social media has done is enable us to build relationships quicker, sort the wheat from the chaff and then nurture those relationships.

Researching

There are many ways you can approach companies about your solutions and services. The most popular over the last 30 years were mail shots and cold calling. I mention them together as they are tied in terms of measurement.

When I started selling, this approach was described to me as the 'girls at a dance' approach. Which was, if I went to a disco and wanted to dance with a girl, all I had to do was to ask every girl in the room as one would say yes. I wanted to say, surely you try to find the girl most likely to say yes, through open questioning, but I didn't, as I could see this would be career limiting.

Thirty years ago when I started work we had a typing pool and I gave letters to them to type; each one had to be individually crafted and they got a pretty good response. Then came word processors and word processing software and the belief was that if we could create more and more direct mail (DM) then we would get a better and better response. Then came e-mail and we switched from DMs to sending as many e-mails as we could. Why? We no longer need to pay for postage and an e-mail is 'free' after all. Our only restriction was the number of people's e-mail addresses we had. There is now a whole industry based on how to write headers that will get people to open these e-mails rather than just delete them. As soon as we moved into mass DM and e-mails, we had to write based on the lowest common denominator to try to appeal to as many people as we could. Technology was developed to catch these e-mails before they 'filled up' your inbox. Junk folders and rules on incoming e-mails were all created to help you manage these e-mails and stop them cluttering up your day.

The same goes for telesales or telemarketing. We just call out, call upon call using 'technology' to make it easier for the agents. Scripts dumb down the messaging and try to trick the prospective customer into saying yes. Software will automatically dial out before the conversation has stopped so that agents can make more and more call outs. Technology such as voice mail was also created to help executive assistants keep away these cold callers. Laws had to be passed to stop salespeople calling certain telephone numbers.

All of this meant companies had to 'throw more and more mud at the wall and hope it will stick'. If at any time DMs or cold calling aren't deemed to work, you just increase the number of calls or DMs. Sales is a numbers game after all.

The likelihood your unsolicited e-mail will be read is around 4 per cent, which is a 96 per cent rejection rate. The likelihood your LinkedIn InMail will be read is approximately 7 per cent, which is a 93 per cent rejection rate. I'm not sure about you but I'm not big on rejection, so what can I do to get rejection rates of maybe just 10 per cent?

Account-based marketing (ABM), also known as key account marketing, is a strategic approach to business marketing in which an organization considers and communicates with individual prospects or customer accounts as markets of one. It parallels the movement of business-to-consumer marketing away from mass marketing, where organizations try to sell individual products to as many new prospects as possible, to 1:1 marketing.

Let's not get too carried away here as there are readers that will have multiple accounts. We are not saying you should just focus on one account. The idea is to increase your personalization to focus in on an account and individuals in that account. Like when Jon started the conversation with me about my favourite vinyl record, we want the approach to be appropriate and authentic, with context to that individual.

My friend Paul (the one getting 10 C-level meetings a week using Twitter) is doing just that. He runs a networking company, bringing C-level people together. But if you think about it, as individuals, once we have been to his meetings, twice, we also have the network as we have met the people we want at the meetings. To get people to come back, he has to provide great content. He's always looking for great speakers.

When Twitter launched its Periscope product, which allows you to live stream video to Twitter, Paul hit on the idea of getting the head of Periscope to speak at one of his events, as that would be a great audience draw. He then went away to research the head of Periscope at Twitter. Now he could have sent the guy a template e-mail, probably like all the other template e-mails that people get. Instead he researched the guy online and created a 'Word Swag' using the app, and within an hour the guy had come back, they had a DM conversation on Twitter, and he agreed to speak at an event. Paul tells me he has a 90 per cent acceptance rate with Word Swags.

More details on the application Word Swag and an example of it are provided in Chapter 8.

Now before somebody thinks, I know, I'll create one Word Swag and e-mail it out to everybody, the key is that one-to-one personalization gets a lower rejection rate.

So let's go back to Paul and his approach to the human resources director. He used standard ABM techniques on her, couldn't find her on Twitter and LinkedIn but did find her on Instagram. On finding her interest in cats, he created a Word Swag with a cat photo and a quote and contacted her. It was highly personalized. From creating that connection and building the rapport he was able to connect with her on LinkedIn, enabling him to nurture that relationship.

For example, any HR-related content that he posts on LinkedIn or likes, she will be able to see. This helps to continue to build and nurture his relationship and his leadership position in her eyes and also brings her into his community. Hopefully she will 'like' or 'retweet' some of his content, which will then ripple through her network. This amplifies what Paul is saying, but it may well also get picked up by other HR directors, who may then follow Paul as they may be interested in more of that content, thus expanding Paul's network and community. They may even like or retweet it, expanding Paul's network and community even further.

Talking

At the beginning of this chapter we discussed the need in social media to talk to strangers. But in a room of 100 people, how do we get to those 20 people we need to know, quicker? Then we considered the fact that we shouldn't just jump in and start trying to sell, but should listen to what our prospects and customers are interested in. Then we should try to build rapport and engagement with them around subject areas they understand or are passionate about, thus building trust and context, but also being authentic at the same time.

The next part of this chapter discusses how we can talk with prospects, customers and influencers using the techniques we have learnt so far.

When people ask my advice on Twitter, I also say the first thing to do on Twitter is not to tweet but listen. Many of us were taught at school that 'good behaviour' was writing pages and pages. The longer the essay, the better.

Social media requires you to write in short sentences, as a summary of what you want to say. This art, like many social media techniques, has been around for years; the art of the headline writer. Journalists and their subeditors needed to get you to read their article. The way they did this was to write a headline that would draw you in. Some people call it a hook. It's about drawing you in so you spend time reading what has been written.

When we read a newspaper, we don't read what we perceive as boring articles. If somebody looks boring we avoid them. So don't be boring.

In addition, don't be a 'corporate suit'. I know it's tempting to tweet or post on LinkedIn articles your company wants you to post. But come on. If you think they are boring, so will your audience. If your audience thinks they are boring then people won't follow you – they will in fact avoid you. Just like the person at the networking drinks who wants to talk about his double glazing, people will avoid you too.

Employee advocacy seems to be coming into fashion with big corporates right now. Your customers and prospects are not going to believe what your employees say, as they will also read the company material and say 'Of course they are going to say that, they work there'. So while your employees are a great way to increase your 'share of voice' (this is a measurement of how much muck you throw at the wall) nobody will listen and more importantly nobody trusts what the employees say. But the big thing that corporations like is the ability to control the message. Later on in the book we will talk about social media maturity models and how corporations have to let go of the message for customers and prospects to test it. The more corporations lose control, the more customers and prospects will trust them. This is a scary position that corporations are still trying to grapple with.

Previously in this chapter we have discussed how to approach strangers and accounts to research them and offer a personalized message. This approach moves away from 'spray and pray' to invest in time to focus on an individual to understand them before engaging. Just like we would if we sat opposite them in their office.

By using active listening, we can also work with prospects, customers and influencers and personalize the message more. The more we personalize the less rejection we get.

This is particularly relevant when approaching influencers. Don't forget an influencer can make or break you. A clumsy approach could be tweeted for the whole world to see.

I recall a call with a senior social selling professional when they itemized their strategy. What would happen was an e-mail would go out to each salesperson each day with a list of influencers in their area. It would be the salesperson's job to make contact with the influencer and offer them a piece of their content. My immediate thought was absolute horror. In the early days of the social selling project, we would let people with little or no social presence make contact with seriously influential people, enquiring about the likeability of a certain product with back-up of a boring corporate white paper. (Note: nobody reads white papers anymore.) This was a disaster in the making.

Contacting influencers is straightforward if you use the techniques mentioned above. You need influencers in your community as this helps to validate your brand and will bring you amplification and growth. You always need to talk to strangers but you should also see organic growth, just like when you go to a networking event. The group that is laughing the most is the group people want to be part of. Successful communities will breed success.

If you want to connect with an influencer, don't just bound up to them like Tigger in Winnie the Pooh. Influencers will want a personalized message just like everybody else. Use your best active listening techniques. Read the material they write and when you connect with them, sell them the parts you like best of all. For example, tell them 'I've read your blog and can really relate with the Networking event theme'.

Influencers are always looking for good content, so if you have some great research or a great infographic or both, then why not share with them? Don't be offended if they don't respond or don't think it's great – you can always try with something else another time. Don't forget influencers are not sitting there waiting for your approach; they are busy people trying to make a living like all of us.

My advice is not to approach them and say, 'I've got a great website, what do you think?', or 'I've got a great app, what do you think?' We probably get three or four of those approaches a day individually. It's not original and just passes into the general noise of everything else. Think about it, is that personalized? Why do you switch into sales mode as soon as you have made contact? Why would I or anybody trust you?

A sales guy from Social Bro approached me by retweeting a few of my blogs, offered me feedback as to which ones he liked best, and even suggested a few areas he would like to see me explore. We would have frequent chats, and I even met him and helped him with some personalized e-mails he wanted to send. It was at that meeting (I knew it was coming) where he pitched Social Bro to me. I would have, if I was him. He even had a 'sympathy close'. Even though Social Bro is a 'social' company they still used telesales to sell. He wanted to show to his bosses you can use Social to make a sale.

In the bonus material we talk about how to deal with inbound enquiries. If you are networking, sharing and engaging, people will spot you and hopefully be curious to look further as to who you are. In many cases these people are 'lurkers' or they do want something but are often too shy to make contact. One trick I use is that everybody that comes to my LinkedIn profile gets a note thanking them for making the effort to look at my profile and asking if they need any help. I have experimented with mentioning my blog, but actually keeping the message simple gets the best response. Maybe keeping it simple drives them to a conversation rather than suggesting they move elsewhere.

Of all the messages I send out I get a 50 per cent response rate. Sometime it is 'you popped up in my network', and often they want to connect so they can keep up with my posts. It has also got me many opportunities in terms of podcast invites, which always allows me to grow my reach into other people's communities and networks.

Summary

In this chapter we have looked at how many of the life skills we gained in the offline world can be used in the online world. How going to a dance or a networking event can help us as we continue on our social media journey. Making contact with people we don't know can turn them into contacts, prospects, customers and advocates. Better still they help us create a community that we can sow and harvest to enable us to create leads and revenue.

Controlling influence

04

The objective of this chapter is to examine how influence works in social networks, and how the reader can manipulate influence in order to attract customers.

What is influence?

In this chapter we're going to look in depth at the idea of influence, and why it's so important with regards to your social selling efforts.

Influence is one of those words that is mentioned a lot in terms of social networks and social media, but what influence actually is predates those technologies and goes all the way back to the start of commerce itself. 'Influencing', from a commercial perspective at least, is what a marketer does to an individual to make them reach into their pocket and pay for your service.

Throughout the last 30 years the advertising industry has chosen celebrities to promote products. The reason for this is that being recognizable as a celebrity drives influence.

In essence, if a celebrity 'backs' something (like Fairy Liquid, or BT, or Cadbury's, and so on), we are more likely to ape that behaviour. We've used the word 'ape' deliberately here because this harks back, sociologically speaking, to tribal behaviour where we are hard wired to follow the behaviour of our peers that we deem to be successful. We've already discussed how, back when we were living in caves, our tribes were small and static. We'd follow the behaviour of the alpha male/alpha female because we could see what they were doing was successful. Using celebrities in marketing in this way taps into this hard-wired behaviour. We tend to frame celebrities as 'alphas' (which is why we celebrate them), and hence we tend to follow.

In the pre-social networking days, using celebrities in this way was a top-down approach using television adverts to broadcast messages, looking to influence the behaviour of customers. It worked pretty well because there was far less distraction – in the UK there were only four channels, only two of which carried adverts, and no Twitter, Facebook, texting, etc to distract people.

Today in 2016, things are very different. But the idea of using celebrities to hack hard-wired tribal behaviour in terms of influence still works, it just depends how you define what a 'celebrity' is.

Your celebrity

In the example above, we were talking about how celebrities were used in television ads to influence the market. Television ads were and are all about B2C (Business to Consumer) selling, and in this book we're mostly interested in B2B (Business to Business) selling. However, ideas around celebrity are still important for Business to Business.

A celebrity for the purposes of our discussion is someone who can influence others without 'touching' them. Most of us as salespeople can influence people to buy from us by going out, meeting with them, and selling to them. We are influencing their behaviour away from choosing a competitor and towards choosing us. In this process we can be said to be 'touching' the person because we are interacting with them. We have a relationship with the customer. A celebrity can do that same job of influencing behaviour away from choosing a competitor and choosing us without having that relationship.

In reality, that relationship is implied. When we, and we all do this, 'celebrate' a celebrity, at some level we believe we know them and have a relationship with them because from a purely sociological perspective we only really understand our relationships with people as if we were in a cave and living in a tribe. In other words, if they are in our lives we have to at some level know them.

The advantage of being a salesperson who has celebrity status with the customers is that you can achieve greater scale. We could all, with infinite time and money, go out and meet every individual in the market, 'touch' them, form one-to-one relationships and sell. We don't have infinite time and money – but we can gain celebrity and in this way bring customers to us, without us having to touch them.

In the first chapter we spoke about why it was important to frame your social selling efforts around the idea of community. The reason we need a community is because it becomes the centre of our influence. However, that's only the start of the work we have to do, as the job of manipulating influence to our own advantage is complex and multifaceted.

Let's take a diversion to talk about a key example of influence – YouTubers.

YouTubers

If you have kids, you'll be aware that they don't watch TV. You can hardly get them interested in films anymore. If you're going to see them watch anything, it's almost certainly YouTube. Most likely they'll be watching people playing Minecraft. Or more specifically, they'll be watching people 'playing with ideas around the concept of Minecraft'. That distinction is quite important.

What kids tend to watch on YouTube are not funny cat videos. They are generally not watching clip shows, compilations of 'You've Been Framed' or 'America's Funniest Home Movies'. What they are watching generally are 'YouTubers'. These are people who have their own channels, their own identities, but they tell stories and make programmes that look almost nothing like what older generations would consider a TV programme to be.

One such example is Stampy Cat. He has a series on his channel called 'Stampy's Lovely World'. He updates it weekly, and has been doing so for many years. In it, he builds things in Minecraft. Each week in his world he'll build a shop, or a house, or a game, and he'll explain how he's doing it. And his fans will watch him do this, for 20 minutes a week. The video he made in December 2015 had around

750,000 views. That's three-quarters of a million kids who have watched him in a week. And they'll come back the next week to watch him do the next one.

For kids, YouTube has replaced television. YouTubers like Stampy Cat, iBallisticSquid, and Dan DTM have become celebrities who have tremendous influence over these children.

Peculiarly though, none of these YouTubers try to overtly sell to their audience. For example, none of them take a break 10 minutes in and say, 'Hey kids... Hmmm... I'm a bit thirsty. Time for a delicious Coke Zero!' They all could, and I'd imagine Coca-Cola inc. would love to give them money to do it, but for some reason they don't and that reason appears to be more sociological than driven by regulations or ethics. It's more that it doesn't occur to a 20-year-old or younger YouTuber to do that, as opposed to there being some structural reason why it's impractical.

Aspiration works differently too in this context. Traditional 'Mad Men' advertising works through aspiration – drink this drink and the opposite sex will be desperate to go to bed with you, and so on. For YouTubers, the aspiration is that the viewer will become better at what they like doing. By watching this video, little Johnny knows how to kill the Ender Dragon, or build a model of a Creeper, or how to build a specific widget out of 'red stone'.

In the new world of celebrities that can influence B2C behaviour via their YouTube channels and community we see connected economy behaviour squeezing out commercial and corporate behaviour. Specifically we see that 'karmic, free exchange of ideas for the benefit of the whole group' behaviour that we've discussed throughout so far. Or to put it more simply, 'we're not here to sell to you, we're here to do something we enjoy as a group'.

(That's not to say there isn't commercial influence over this new world. When the new LEGO Dimensions game was being released, all the YouTubers had the game and all the support they needed to push the message out to potential consumers in their communities.)

The reason why we have to understand YouTubers is because they portend what B2C celebrities will become as the current generation gets older and 'Generation Television' dies off. Specifically, celebrities become people who build up large communities of followers, and deliver valuable insights and information. Therefore, when we're looking at becoming a celebrity ourselves within our own little B2B domain, that's the angle that we need to approach it from.

The structure of influence

It's helpful to understand what we need to do in terms of moulding pre-existing influence in our target market. Whatever market you are in, there will be pre-formed opinions and existing players. We have two jobs to do. First, our own influence needs to increase. Second, the influence of others who are not helpful to us needs to decrease. Controlling influence is also a constant process. We like to think of it as a little like moving around and shaping wet sand. We need to get it where we want it, and form a shape with it. But over time the shape will tend to fall back to being a shape we don't want. But it's very important that you consider that influence is valuable to both you and your competitors. Similarly, gaining influence is a slow, careful process that has to be done constantly (although it's fair to say that once you have a critical mass of influence, it becomes hard for others to dislodge that).

Competitors are generally more important in social selling than most people realize. Although the principles of social selling are based on warm and fluffy connected economy ideas, the reality is that you still need to win, and that in order to win you need a certain amount of aggression focused on your competitors. Most people don't do that, so a very easy advantage is available to you simply by being aware of who your competitors are and watching or listening to their activities. We'll talk far more about that later.

'Competitors' in this context is generally broader than your traditional commercial competitors. It's anyone who has influence over your customers. There will be non-commercial 'actors' in your space who have influence. Plus, there will be new disruptive ideas and/or technologies that will also have influence.

There are generally six groups of personas that you need to consider:

1 your social community manager (SCM), sales staff, marketing staff and others;

2 your SCM's counterpart and ancillaries at your competitors';

3 'loved-up' influencers who advocate your offerings;

4 'loved-up' influencers who advocate competing offerings;

5 paid influencers who advocate your offerings;

6 paid influencers who advocate competing offerings.

FIGURE 4.1 The structure of influence

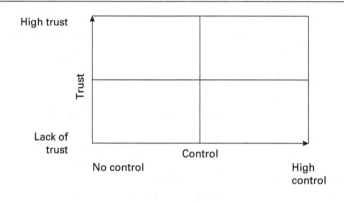

You can see that there are broadly two types of persona – those who advocate your offerings, and those who advocate competing offerings. Our objective is to make the people on our side more efficient, and to make the people who aren't on our side less efficient. Again, to reiterate, it's important you do both those things.

Cutting across horizontally, we have three types of persona:

1 SCMs and ancillaries;

2 'loved-up' influencers;

3 paid influencers.

SCMs and their ancillaries we have discussed at length already, but in this context their job is to build influence. This means they need to become celebrities in their own right within your chosen domain. In this way, they will be able to attract customers cold (ie customers will just come to them), and they'll be able to sway customers who are being engaged by competitors. In reality, it's likely the SCM will become the celebrity and the ancillaries (salespeople, marketing team, and the rest of the business) will act as supports to that key person.

Again, we need to consider the competitors. Over time they will want their SCMs to be the leading celebrity within your shared domain. We'll talk more about competitor SCMs later, but one obvious tactic here is that if your competitor's SCM does become really good, you can always poach them. The flip side of course is that they can poach yours.

All of these various actor types that we're talking about have a different way in which trust and control operates. You have ultimate control over what your SCM does because they work for you. You therefore don't have to trust them very much, in that they are unlikely to do anything unhelpful to you as a business. (An SCM is almost never going to promote a white paper saying how amazing your competitors are and how useless you are – you can inherently trust them not to do that.)

The next type of persona is the 'loved-up' people. These are individuals who behave in what is easy to regard as quite a peculiar way – they will spend their own time, effort and money promoting a commercial product or service just because they like it. Importantly, they do not work for a vendor in the space. All they want to do is talk about how amazing XYZ technology is, and they'll end up with so many followers that even their dog has 50,000 followers and is regarded as an expert in its own right.

These people are the YouTubers of B2B commercial influence space. They are classic connected economy individuals, sharing ideas and talking to people just because they want everyone to improve, and they don't particularly want to be paid for doing it.

Loved-up personas are particularly dangerous because you have no control over them. Therefore your trust in them has to be very little. They might spend years promoting your product only for you to find out one day they hate you and have fallen in love with your competitor, with all the attendant influence flowing from you to your competitor.

To the customer, loved-up influencers are highly attractive because they have no (perceived) bias. As we said right back in the introduction, customers operate in salesperson avoidance mode and hate bias. Loved-up influencers are therefore manna from heaven to customers. Which is another way of saying 'you need them', and we'll talk below about how to get them.

The final type of persona is paid persons. These can be in two forms – loved-up actors who are being motivated with a cheque, or the effective equivalent of 'celebrity endorsements', ie people who are not paid-up members of the community, but who can fly in and say something to the community without being part of it.(Imagine Danny Dyer being paid to say something nice about XYZ plc's hosted telephony solution. Danny Dyer can be anyone here so long as they are generally recognizable to the community – they don't have to be a 'featured in Hello magazine'-type celebrity.)

In our opinion, paid influencers don't particularly work well. They are what someone who understands old-school advertising goes to when they think they want influencers – they pay someone recognizable to carry the banner for them. As discussed, customers don't like bias and they can sniff out bias in paid advocates a mile away.

Legal implication

It is worth mentioning the legal implication of paid influence here. In the United States, for example, you need to identify if you are being paid to recommend something, and even if it isn't a legal requirement we think it's considered ethical in sales and social generally.

Given that we have these six actor types, we need to move each of them around so that they are more helpful to us, and less helpful to our competitors. To reiterate, this is a constant process so it's not a case of doing this exercise once and then forgetting about it:

- For our SCM and ancillaries, the idea is that they do not move around, but instead just get better at what they do.
- For our competitor's SCM and ancillaries, we can overtly move them by poaching them, but practically what we need to do is leave them where they are, but just make sure we remain better than them.

- For our loved-up influencers, the objective is to get a little more control over what they say. Ultimately this may mean turning them into paid advocates, or actually hiring them.

- For our competitor's loved-up influencers, the objective is to transform them into being our loved-up influencers, our paid advocates, or to hire them.

- For our paid influencers – this depends on how they have come about. The objective here would be to leave them where they are, or bring them in-house.

- For our competitor's paid influencers – the option here is to outbid your competitors, or hire them.

What we're trying to show here is that this is a dynamic system, and that ideally you want to get into a position where you have some say in who goes where. What you don't want is to sit idly by whilst your competitor farms a collection of loved-up influencers selling their products, especially when you could be doing that yourself.

How do you create loved-up influencers?

It will be tempting to think that you can create loved-up influencers from scratch. It's obviously appealing to have people out there actively promoting your product for you, expecting virtually nothing in return, so why would you not take positive action to create more of those sorts of people?

Whilst it's certainly essential to 'lock in' loved-up influencers, and bring them closer so they don't become 'disloyal', creating them from scratch is almost certainly a non-starter. It takes a very special, and dare I say unique individual, to love a product so much that they end up being a loved-up influencer. You won't find them. It's far better to concentrate on scaling your efforts as per everything else we've been describing in this chapter.

Control and trust

The different personas that we're talking about all have a different profile when it comes to control and trust. Understanding those profiles is hugely important when it comes to balancing risk in and growth of your community.

Your community is a business investment, so ideally you want to have total or near-total control over it, much as you would any other asset. Specifically, you want to control every message, every conversation, and so on. However, in terms of the people in your community there are only two classes that you can control – your SCM and ancillaries, and paid advocates.

If your community is only those people, you cannot scale. You can only achieve 'social scale' by giving up control. (Just to continue this for a moment, 'going viral' is the ultimate in achieving social scale for a given message, but when this happens you lose control entirely.)

Let me give you a real-world example. In a previous life I used to be a 'loved-up' advocate for Microsoft. They never paid me any actual money, but over my time with them I used to get special treatment and 'treats', as a reward for me helping software developers understanding how to use Microsoft products to build software. I managed to gain quite a following, and for a good while this worked really well for both of us.

Then two things happened. First, I got a gig writing for the *Guardian*'s technology section. This took me from having a reasonable following in a niche market (software developers) to a massive following in a general market (anyone in the western world interested in technology). Second, they released what was widely perceived as a disappointing product: Windows 8. Overnight they went from having someone being a loved-up advocate entirely on message, to having someone attacking a much more important product to a much, much larger audience. From their perspective this must have been shocking.

From my perspective I was doing the right thing – I spent some time honestly and frankly talking about how good some of their products were, and then I was presented with a new product, which in my opinion was terrible, and spoke honestly and frankly about that. The point is that they had virtually no control over me.

If you have an employee or outside supplier working within the community, you can control everything they do. If an employee sends something out of message, you can take them to one side and, essentially, make them delete it and/or make them take steps to control the damage (ideally, at least). But if someone in your community you have no control over does something you don't like, your only option is damage control.

The solution to this problem is 'relationships'. Given my example above, what could Microsoft have done to stop me writing pieces in the *Guardian* that eviscerated their new product? Well, they could have asked me to stop writing and work with them on making it better.

Essentially it's your job as someone who owns a community to be able to bring people 'into the fold' where you can notch up the control you have over what they are saying. This works in both a proactive and a reactive way. Proactively, by educating key members of your community as to what you are doing and why keeps them on message. Reactively, having a closer relationship with those people means you're able to contact them and gently encourage them back on message. But you need to consider that, as we know, prevention is generally better than cure.

Returning to Figure 4.1 again (see page 64), this diagram shows how trust tails off as we give up control. The important thing to remember is that it's a necessity to give up control in order to achieve scale.

Modelling

Social selling has a sneaky secret, in that everything you do, your competitors can watch you do. The nature of social networks is that the activities are all performed out in the open. So, whereas your competitors might not know that internally you're running a telesales campaign to poach all of their business, if you do that same thing on social networks they certainly could notice it.

The flipside to this is that when your competitor is running a social selling campaign to poach your customers, you should spot them doing that too. Or to put it another way, the rules of the game are the same for both sides – everything happens out in the open, and that means there is a lot of information out there that you can take advantage of.

We've spoken about the importance of listening – now we come to talk about the importance of modelling this as a type of applied listening, which we discussed in Chapter 3.

This is where personality, having a social profile that is authentic but also human (through engagement) really pays off because even if your competitor is doing similar things it will be about the relationship you have built and invested in over time

If you consider a given individual on a social network, they will have their own little universe of people that they talk to, and things they talk about. They also have a list of people they follow, and a list of people who follow them. This information is almost always public, because the networks fundamentally want you to see this information and trace down and follow paths of people who you think are similar to yourself. (We talk more about how social networks work in Chapter 5, and we spoke about this idea of tribalism in Chapter 1.)

If you also look at what people post, you can get a very good idea of their interests. They will usually have two types of interests – core interests, and niche interests. These themselves will subdivide into professional and personal interests, although for many people these are blended. For example, is my interest in 'entrepreneurship' personal or professional? It's probably both. However, you'll also see me (for reasons I've never fully understood) tweet about McDonald's a lot. Hey, I like McDonald's – don't judge! I don't own a McDonald's franchise, so that's a personal interest for me.

The point is that by using the account-based marketing ideas that we've already discussed, you can build up a picture of an individual just by looking at their activity. You can use this picture to determine what they are doing, as well as how they are doing it. For example, if you examine the behaviour of a salesperson at a competing firm and see them striking up conversations with CTOs (Chief Technology Officers) of non-profit/charity organizations, and trying to close them on downloading a white paper, you can infer that they are running a certain campaign and using a long-form content marketing strategy as part of that campaign.

You can then determine what you want to do about that. You can leave them to it, or you can actively work to ameliorate the potential success of their campaign in some way. For example, if you see someone engaging with a competitor's white paper, that individual is telegraphing that they are a good lead. Your agility here will be important in terms of which tactics you adopt, and we'll talk about this in later chapters.

The idea of using an account-based marketing technique to research people that you want to engage with has an obvious advantage – it's easier to engage with someone when you have some idea about who they are, and what they want. However, what we're suggesting here is that you scale this out in a structured way, and create a 'model' of your market comprising products, customers, competitors, partners and suppliers.

The company that has the best model will win – simple as that. A model is a representation of your market, and it's self-evident that the company that understands its market best will be the most successful.

Summary

In this chapter we have discussed the importance of influence and why you need to get some in the digital economy. The debate has moved on from personal branding; this is not enough to differentiate you anymore. Salespeople and marketers reading this, you must not underestimate the need to own your market. You might not be a thought leader but you can control your influence.

Creating and controlling influence within your own territory/community will mean that prospects and changemakers will be attracted to you, which will in turn create inbound enquiries direct to you.

The mechanics
of traditional
sales

05

In this chapter we're going to look at the actual mechanics of social networks. Some readers may find this chapter a little technical, but it's worth powering through, as understanding the mechanism by which the market operates will help you to ultimately find opportunities and leads.

We'll start by looking at the mechanics of traditional B2B telesales. This typically works by a salesperson having a list of people to call ('interrupt', really), and then working through that list methodically. Some proportion of calls will turn into conversations. Some conversations turn into meetings. Some meetings turn into leads. Some leads turn into opportunities. Ultimately, some opportunities turn into sales.

That process is very easy for anyone to understand. Each stage involves taking a set of 'n' things in at the top, doing some operation to each thing, and ending up with a group of things that are discarded (people who wouldn't return calls, flat out rejected the offer, etc), and a group of things that are kept and progressed on (people who did agree for meetings).

Typically, managing this process involves conceptualizing the process as a funnel, a funnel being particularly appropriate because at each stage the set of things we're working at is whittled down as we progress to the next stage. It's also possible to statistically analyse the sales operation such that either at a team level or an individual level, we know that a given set at any stage will likely reduce by a known given proportion. Most salespeople either intuitively understand, or alternatively actively manage around those statistics: 'I need to make 20 calls a day, 100 per week, to get five meetings'. Sales is a numbers game, salespeople often say.

The important part here is that it's easy for everyone to understand that if you stop running that process, you stop getting a useful end result. Or more clearly, if you don't make calls, you don't get meetings. (Or at least the meetings you do get arrive serendipitously because of prior actions – eg having a good relationship with a customer who moves to another company and finds an opportunity for you there that you hadn't explicitly chased down.)

There are also a number of very visible and very obvious supporting activities to this process. If a salesperson needs to call 100 people a week, they need a list of those 100 people. If a salesperson needs to attend a meeting, they need time to prepare, attend the meeting, transport to get there, etc.

Traditional B2B sales in this way is in reality highly mechanistic. Moreover, the structure of 'sales machines' like this is old but efficient, and is still prevalent in sales teams regardless of their industry. This means that whoever the salesperson works for and in what industry, the process is: make calls, set meetings, nurture opportunities, close deals.

In social selling, where we're using networking techniques on social networks to find leads and make sense, we're right at the beginning of the adoption curve, and so the equivalent 'sales machine' for social selling is still a work in progress. This is a good thing because it allows you to help design that machine (and that brings attendant opportunities and rewards), but also a bad thing in that there's no obvious way to build such a machine.

A quick word on technology adoption curves

The technology curve or 'adoption lifecycle' depicted in Figure 5.1 is used as a way of explaining people's adoption of new products or services. People's adoption styles will influence which approach/tactic you will need to employ to sell your product or service.

Innovators, you know the type, are the ones with the latest iPhone and always seem to battle through the technical glitches of a "version

FIGURE 5.1 Technology adoption lifecycle

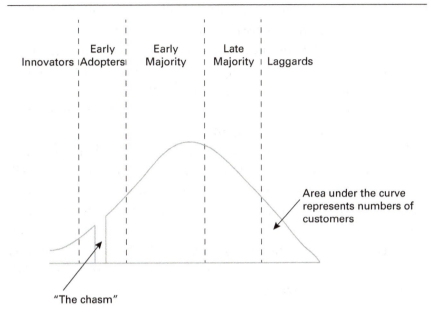

one" product. Then come the early adopters, who like to see use cases before they will adopt technology, but still adopt it early on. The early majority are the greatest proportion of people; the iPhone is arguably now at this stage as so many people use it. Those people who are slower to adopt a new technology are the late majority or laggards.

The mechanics of networking

We've said throughout this book that social selling is much more like networking than traditional sales. Whilst structurally there is a great deal of overlap in this scenario, there is an important difference as to what networking events are actually for.

There are some salespeople who do all their selling through traditional networking. However, this process doesn't necessarily look that different to traditional sales. We'll call 'traditional networking' (ie the type where you turn up in a room and there is tea and coffee) 'IRL networking', or 'in-real-life networking'.

From a mechanistic point of view, IRL networking replaces just the list-building part of traditional sales, and softens initial interactions.

Someone who attends IRL networking will collect business cards, and then look to develop the initial meet by calling or e-mailing to set up meetings where further discussions can be held. Thus far when we've spoken about the networking analogy, we've asked you to concentrate on the fact that the process of collecting business cards ('list building') has to be done using a listen-wait-interact method.

Where this analogy breaks down is that salespeople at an IRL networking event are still primarily there to sell.

That is not the case with social selling, where the salesperson's primary job is to build trust relationships and authority, and not to sell. Again looking at the mechanics, someone attending an IRL networking event is not traditionally operating in 'salesperson avoidance mode', typically because they themselves are salespeople and IRL networking is structured as a 'sales event'. They are an extension of traditional sales that has come about primarily to make list-building activities more efficient.

The mechanics of social networks

So what are people on a social network there for if it's not to buy and sell? Well, the clue is in the name: they are there to be 'social'. This is why we have stressed that you have to be perceived as being useful to people on the network. You do this by being a supplier of timely information, which in itself delivers value, as opposed to just a supplier of goods and services. By building up a community and building up authority around the 'domain' of that community, you are able to create value.

All three types of system – traditional telesales, IRL networking, and social networking – have one thing in common, which is that in order for it to work you have to do something. If you don't make phone calls, you don't get meetings. If you don't go to an IRL networking event, you don't get meetings. If you don't interact on social networks, you don't get meetings.

In each of these systems, by doing something you are creating 'resonance'. Imagine you go to an art gallery. You go into a room and people are in there looking at the art, talking amongst themselves, etc. Now imagine you stand in the middle of the room and ring a bell.

Everyone will turn and look at you. If you go into the room and don't ring a bell, it's unlikely anyone would notice you.

When on social networks, it is essential that you create resonance in some way. Everyone on a social network is having their attention attracted by something – your job is to be the one who attracts it.

Integration with the sales funnel

It's important to remember that whatever you do on the social networks has to feed into your sales funnel. In order to transition people from your social network into your sales funnel, you have to be having private conversations. Essentially, what we are doing is replacing the list building and interruption aspects of the traditional sales process with social networking activities.

People do not discuss their needs – ie your leads – publicly (or at least it's very unlikely that they will). To get people to disclose leads, you have to meet with them privately. This means going through a process of deepening connections from 'I don't know him/her' to 'I'm meeting him/her for coffee next week'.

Your objective throughout all this is to drive people through to a point where you are having meetings.

Follower/following

Most social networks operate on a follower/following model. You have some identity in the network, you follow people with a similar identity who you are interested in, and ultimately other people will follow you because they are interested in you too.

It's interesting that LinkedIn doesn't quite fit into this model, yet a follower/following model is still essentially the definition of a social network. Twitter, Facebook, and others like Snapchat and Instagram use the model. LinkedIn's directory approach predates this more modern social network structure.

It's generally true to say that the bigger the set of people following you, the better your performance on social networks will be. This is because the bigger the set of people following you, the 'louder' your bell will be when you ring it.

You'll find that this is generally known as 'reach'. We're not going to use that term here particularly because, for us, the metaphor is the wrong way around. You are looking to do something that attracts attention, and 'reach' implies you're physically going out there and 'reaching out' and touching people to get their attention.

When you post an article on a social network, if you have 10 followers it will only appear on 10 people's timelines. If you have a thousand followers, it will appear on a thousand people's timelines. In that sense, having a bigger set of followers is obviously good.

Some people will say that you need to consider 'quality over quantity'. This isn't true. As long as you don't buy followers, an organically built list will have value that is to all practical intents and purposes proportionate with its size. Arguments like 'I have 10,000 followers!' 'Yes, but how many of those are quality followers?' are essentially navel gazing.

Ultimately you will have two motivations here. You will generally want to build the size of your follower set, because having a bigger set is better. However, you will also have certain people that you want to have relationships with. Let's say you want to sell into XYZ plc. You will go and find people on the network from XYZ plc as part of your account-based marketing (ABM) efforts. You have to be more proactive and definite in getting these people to follow you, and from there to have private conversations with you. However, the principles remain the same, whether you are targeting specific people or the general population.

Let's look at the other side for a moment – what motivates someone to add someone to the 'followings' set?

People follow people on social networks primarily because those followings deliver value back to the 'follower'. To stretch the bell-ringing analogy, it's better to have a set of followers whose bell ringing is like a nice campanological music as opposed to a deafening cacophony of off-key notes. What a follower is looking to do is have a set of followings that propagates ideas and information that is aligned with the follower's objectives. The follower will always drive efficiency around that point.

To be clear, having a bunch of spammy salespeople in their followings set does not create efficiency for the follower. Having a salesperson who's a leader in their community and is sharing practical information does create efficiency.

At this point you, the salesperson, want to be in as many individual following sets as possible. You already have some followers, and you want to have more. So, you need to 'ring your bell'. This is done by creating 'signals' in the network, as we'll now explain.

Signals

Signals are typically expressed as notifications by the network. If you follow someone, that person will see a notification saying that you have followed them. This is a signal – it's the 'sound waves' from your bell reaching them. The point is that it increases the chances that they will follow you. If you're just sitting there in the network doing nothing, there is a chance that individual will find you and follow you (but that chance is very, very small). However, by proactively following them, and in doing so creating a signal, the chance of them following you goes up.

You can affect the chance of them following you by providing a better experience when they come to see who you are. This comes down to your messaging around your position, which we discussed earlier. If they come to your profile and it looks likely you will create value for them (ie the efficiency of their followings set will be increased), the chance of them following you is higher.

This is an example of backwards propagation through the network. There are two other ways in which you can do this.

The first is that you can 'favourite' their post. Most networks support the idea of favouriting a post. In 2015, Twitter changed this star to a heart. Much as we think of this branding as form over function ('starring' was just a way of 'pinning' a tweet for future reference or considering; 'loving' it is a whole different thing), the principle remains the same – when you favourite a post the person who posted it is told through a notification. This increases the chance of them checking out your offering and considering you for their followings set.

The second is that you can 'reshare' or 'retweet' their post. The idea of resharing is that you copy their post onto your timeline, but credit them as the original source. Resharing is hugely important, as we'll see when we consider forward propagation in the next section, but in this context someone will see you retweet something through a signal, and again this increases the chances of them checking out your offering and considering you for their followings set.

Backwards propagation is important because it's generally cheap (in terms of effort) and easy.

If you want someone to follow you, make sure your messaging is good and then follow them and favourite some of their posts. The chances of them following you increases if you do that.

Forward propagation

Forward propagation is the single most important factor affecting the growth of your followers set. More than anything, you need to optimize around this.

If you're familiar with Twitter, forward propagation is 'getting retweeted'. Say you have 100 followers and you post something. One of your followers who themselves has 100 followers retweets it. Your message is propagated 'forward' through the network to a greater number of people than is in your followers set. In this example, your message ends up on 200 timelines as opposed to 100.

This is where the term 'reach' does make a little more sense. You are 'reaching' a greater audience of people.

Following that retweet, the followers of this 'retweeter', have received a signal of your existence. The chance that each of those people will check out your offering and follow you has also increased in each instance. But fundamentally this is still all about signals – the more people who see your signals, the more people will check out your offering, and the more people will follow you.

Where this is more valuable than the backward propagation that we just covered is that the value you're sharing gets conveyed forward into the network. If you share a particularly salient or clever idea, as that gets pushed forward the value goes with it. Anyone reading it should say, 'Hmmm, that's a particularly clever/salient idea, who's that smart individual who shared it?', and from there, your association with it (and by implication your authority) also goes forward.

However, there is an association with backwards propagation here in that if you reshare a post of someone else's, that acts as a signal. Coming back to our list of people that we are looking to connect with from an accounts-based marketing (ABM) perspective, by resharing posts of a particular individual, we are actively working towards the goal of having private conversations with them.

Looping this back to the mechanical process of traditional B2B telesales, the same funnel idea applies here. You create signals (old world: a phone call; new world: a posting on a social network), and a proportion of those signals moves the story on (old world: a conversation; new world: a follower).

The value of forward propagation is that it is subject to network effects. The point is that each follower of yours will have (probably) hundreds of followers themselves. And those followers will have hundreds of followers. And it keeps going. The reach (mathematically speaking) into the network can be enormous.

Optimizing around getting forward propagation is either as easy or as difficult as you make it. If you follow the principles of good management of your social network activities (which we cover extensively in this book, but largely can be distilled to: 'put out good quality information and build up authority around a community'), forward propagation should be easy to obtain.

Public conversations

This next part talks about 'engagement', which is also another idea that commonly comes up when talking about social networks.

Engagement is really public conversations, and public conversations are important because they are the last stage before private conversations.

It's very important that you engage with people who engage with you. For example, if you post something and someone has something to say about that post, you need to reply. And that's obvious because if you don't:

a) you're being rude; and

b) everything you have done becomes a waste of effort if you do not talk to them.

Essentially, someone starting a public conversation with you is a huge buying signal as it indicates they have received value from you and want to get more.

When we look at your engagements with others, it comes down to backwards propagation of signals. By initiating a public conversation with someone (eg you see a post of theirs, and comment on it), you're effectively creating a signal much like you do by following them, favouriting their posts, or resharing their content. However, that signal is much more overt, and carries greater cost for you as you have to consider and craft a starting point for the conversation, and then carry the conversation on. That greater effort does have an advantage in that it's a short/shorter hop from public conversations to private ones.

Interestingly, this is where most people struggle when considering how to do social selling, as they consider this aspect of initiating conversations with others as the start of the process. Most people intuitively understand that just spamming out sales messages into social network will not get good results, but then can't balance this tenet with the assumed need to initiate conversations. 'How can I have a conversation with this person I don't know when I can't mention that I'm selling something?'

Of course, this position is impossible. To make social selling work, as hopefully you are seeing by now, you need to overcome this by sowing the seeds of a community, growing that and your attendant authority by building the network using backwards and forwards signal propagation techniques, responding to inbound engagement, and initiating outbound engagement by listening first.

Summary

In this chapter we have seen how in a digital world there are new concepts around following, being followed, retweeted and how these can be used as signals to prospects, customers and competitors. As a social seller you need to use these techniques carefully as you will leave digital footprints wherever you walk online. Once you have mastered this, these techniques are powerful ways for you to own your market and make your numbers.

Moving from an analogue to a social mindset

There are three concepts that were taught to me early in my sales career, that seem to have moved into the digital world.

Every day is a 'school' day – the salespeople that I see winning and making quotas are those that are passionate about their subject. They are effortlessly knowledgeable about customers and the business issues that were solved when their product or service was implemented. These people seem to absorb information like a sponge; in fact they seek it out. These people's attitude is one where they treat every day as a day to seek knowledge, hence the saying that 'every day is a school day'.

PST – Prime Selling Time is the time during the day which you have as a sales professional to sit in front of customers, prospects etc. I was always amazed when a telesales agency I dealt with would book calls with me at 10 am. Surely this is prime selling time for them; it certainly was for me. I would always push the calls back to early in the morning or late in the afternoon.

Making that one extra call – I run calling days, which is where I get the team together for a bit of inter-salesperson competition, and we also compete against other teams. This might not seem fashionable in these days of social and digital but social selling isn't about hiding behind social; you still have to talk with customers. (It's an aside, but we don't do 'interruption' calling – the salespeople will always have warmed the call up through social, marketing automation, etc). There are a number of salespeople that consistently win. These are not the people that treat the day as a chore, a bit like exams, putting off doing any preparation until the last moment when it's too late. The winners spend time preparing, but they are also calling right up to, or even past the time when they should have stopped. You can see that they are making 'just one more call', as it might just well be this one that is the breakthrough. In my career, it is often that extra one where quotas are achieved and beaten.

In today's sales world, the average salesperson will have a mobile phone and therefore, just like their opposite number the buyer, has access to data, 24 hours a day, 365 days a year. The salesperson does not need to be physically present. On planes, trains and (not driving) automobiles, they are connected to the office and sources of data about their products, services, customers and competition.

To be a social seller is not about how much you post and when. It is also not about how much of the company content you can throw at the wall in the hope that it will stick. A social seller is a helper.

Let's take a step back and understand the most important person in our day – the prospect, customer or buyer. A buyer may suddenly be put in a position where they need to research and draw up a short-list of products or services for their company to buy. Let's say filing cabinets. Like me they might not know anything about filing cabinets, so they need to learn. When they make an internal recommendation they will need to explain it. During the education process, they will get to understand their needs better. Do they need two drawer or three drawer cabinets? Will they want cabinets that only take A4 or Foolscap?

One of the things an educated buyer will do is avoid all the people out in the market pushing content that comes across as 'buy my product now' and 'isn't my product amazing'. In fact, that will put off many buyers. But wouldn't it be good if they came across an article: 'The top 10 things you need to think about when buying a filing cabinet'?

Yes, somebody may have embedded in there some of their products' unique selling points (USPs). And the buyer may well say, 'Of course they would say that, they are a filing cabinet selling company'. But the fact you have taken the time to educate the buyer makes it more likely you will get on their shortlist. Better still, you might even get an 'inbound' call, during which you can use your best sales skills to close the buyer before they move onto the competition. As we say, social selling isn't just about playing on social media all day.

This is what we mean by helping the buyer, and you can do this through content marketing. Now any salesperson that has just read that and thought, that is marketing's job, will need to think again.

As a professional salesperson who knows their stuff about filing cabinets, how long would it really take you to write an article about the top 10 things to think about when buying a filing cabinet? An hour, maybe two, then put it on LinkedIn and Twitter as a blog. It might be one of the best demand generation pieces you write, and with a proper thought to SEO (Search Engine Optimization) and a fair wind you might get inbound from it.

Some of the best places for content are your customer and prospect meetings. Good and bad. If you had a meeting with, say, a media company and they outlined their business issues, you would need to type this up and post on the CRM as meeting notes. Why not also turn this into a blog (obviously not mentioning people or companies by name without permission)? Good meetings and bad meetings are ripe for content that you can post out on social media and that will appeal to your typical buyer.

Working with sales teams I often see advice given out by so-called social media gurus that social selling is all about content. Content marketing is the equivalent of talking in the analogue world. Talking with context is fine, but the best thing a salesperson can do is listen. There is an old saying that 'we have been given two ears and one mouth, and we should use them in that order'.

The first thing that a salesperson should do when they want to become a social seller is listen.

Listen to your customers at a macro (company and company executive) level and at a micro level (employees). Listen to your competitors, the analysts, and the trade bodies.

In our roles as trainers of social selling to companies, we came across a sales guy who sells transportation software to supply chain and logistics managers. He had flatlined at 200 followers on Twitter and was getting little engagement. I guessed that the 200 followers were friends and family and he wasn't really getting 'out there'.

'Who's your trade body?', I asked.

'The Chartered Institute of Logistics and Transport Professionals – CILT', was the response.

So I found @CILTUK on Twitter and started paging through their feed. Just by scrolling down I found there was a young person's division, @CILT_YPF. I asked, 'Have you contacted them and asked if you could do an educational presentation?' 'I didn't know they existed', was the response.

@CILT were also retweeting (RTing) a number of thought leaders who were giving presentations. 'Are you talking with these influencers?' 'No, didn't know they existed.'

Each tweet that @CILT had tweeted was a goldmine of how the salesperson could get to know more about their industry and get involved. I pointed out that although you could tell from @CILT's Twitter news feed that it was a 'bot' (automation with no engagement) there was probably a person behind it. I also pointed out that maybe the salesperson might want to engage with that feed, to see if the person would talk back.

We talked in the previous chapter of 'how to talk with strangers' without coming across as weird or spammy. Why not retweet any articles that you think are interesting to your followers? Just by engaging with each of the different people on Twitter will increase your 'interesting' credit and might gain you followers.

We all have 20 minutes while waiting for a train, bus, meeting or sitting in a taxi where we have time for this.

Running some social selling training recently, I had a similar discussion to the one above where the salesperson said, 'Social selling is a waste of time, I cannot increase my following'. I looked at their Twitter feed and said, 'Could it be that you are boring?' 'But I post what the company tell me to post.'

A new follower to us recently contacted me and said, 'I follow you, as what you post is interesting. I don't read every article, but I'm able to build my knowledge by having you in my news feed.'

This is the difference. Your Twitter feed and your LinkedIn profile belong to you. They are a reflection of you and a free advert for you that is online 24 hours a day, 365 days a year. How do you want people to think about you? As a boring corporate suit or as an interesting, funny and vibrant person?

The world has changed and so has the way we need to sell. With buyers online researching your products and services and making recommendations, how are you going to make sure you are found and get on those shortlists?

This means dropping certain 'analogue' habits and getting digital ones. In the old days you may have gone to trade shows, but you need to follow your customers and while you may still attend some trade shows, you need to make sure you are partaking in the digital version too.

As a salesperson you must dedicate time to finding great content in your niche, absorbing it and sharing it on LinkedIn and Twitter. You may have many sources of corporate content, such as colleagues, partners and value-added resellers. 'Jump in' and engage in social; have conversations with colleagues, customers, partners, news sites and social media. Everything ultimately can be repackaged and shared. (We'll talk about specific tools later.)

The world has gone social and so should you. You need to get online and listen; find your customers, competitors and trade bodies and work with them to become the chief of your territory. Winners will be able to manage their time to absorb and create content, not only owning their market but also getting inbound. Nothing could be better than prospects ringing you for help and advice.

So what do you listen for?

All of my salespeople know that whenever we have a territory review, I will always look up the Twitter account or accounts of the companies they're targetting and ask them what the business issues are, or what is impacting those companies today. All of this is publicly available data and on Twitter it is more likely to be up to date than on individual company websites.

In addition, you need to be listening out for signals and using them as a way to get engagement.

Signals – what are they?

Listening (rather than posting) for social sellers is the most important skill in your armoury. So what are you listening for?

The types of signals to look for are dependent on the nature of the product or service you are selling. You need to think about what indicates how a customer or prospect may need your help. It is unlikely that somebody will come onto social media and tweet: '@Timothy_Hughes I need your help', so you need to think laterally.

Every product and service has its own signals but here are the typical ones to look out for:

- organizational change (eg new geography, recruitment drive or redundancies, mergers or acquisitions);
- leadership change;
- market change (eg what is happening to their customers/end users, changes to markets or competition);
- external (eg legislation or regulatory changes, local community news);
- relationship (eg customer, partners, new markets);
- strategic (eg change of direction or focus);
- tactical (eg new initiatives, reviews);
- events (eg newsworthy, sharable events and awards, charitable contributions or sponsorships, incidents or accidents).

Signals

While we can always hope that somebody might tweet your name and ask to buy your product, it is more likely you need to listen on social media, find signals and then interpret them. There are different types of signals to look for on social media, and these can be expanded to cover four main areas.

Relationship

This could be, for example, if a person has won a reward, giving you a reason to connect. The idea is to let them know you are there and not to use this as an excuse to sell. For example, if the CIO of one of your target accounts wins a CIO of the year award, send them a note of congratulations. Do not start talking about your products and services. The congratulations are enough; the fact you represent an organization is enough of an advert.

Risk

It might be that you have picked up in the press that this organization has announced job losses. Still don't sell, but express your sympathy and highlight how you can help and support.

Community

If you understand your prospects, their world and their competition, you can make contact explaining you may have heard an announcement from one of their competitors. Maybe they are expanding, or perhaps they have been fined, and you want to share that with your prospect or customer and express the hope it does not happen to them.

Sales

This is where your prospect has positive news; for example, they are expanding, are part of a merger or acquisition (M&A), have had a change in management or have won a big deal. This gives you the opportunity to position your product as supportive to that news. Note I say 'position', I don't say 'sell'. It's key that you offer a short quantifiable business case and a reference to back it up. It's a pretty good assumption that your target will say, 'Where have you done this before? And what were the results?' before they respond or make contact with you, so be proactive.

Blogs

Blogs are an excellent way to understand the culture and direction of an organization. Three-quarters of B2B marketers are now using blogs as part of their marketing approach.

News

It is often overlooked as a source of insight, but by definition news is information about recent events, and business news is insight into your customers and prospects.

Social media platforms

Join LinkedIn groups that your customers gravitate towards. Monitor Twitter hashtags to identify people and companies that are associated with a particular topic, trend or concept in the markets you serve. Use Glassdoor to give you an insight into what employees think of their company.

Make every minute spent listening a minute well spent.

Here are some examples of LinkedIn social selling triggers you need to look out for:

1   Somebody has viewed your profile, so thank them; we generally get 50 per cent of the people that we contact coming back. This has also turned into business.

2   LinkedIn connect request.

3   Your connection request has been accepted.

4   If your contact changes job, why not congratulate them, or look for a reason to work together and maybe reconnect?

5   Contact gets promoted, see 4 above.

6   Contact's birthday, see 4 above.

7   Contact's work anniversary, see 4 above.

8   Contact is mentioned in the news, see 4 above.

9   Contact updates their profile, so 'like' the update or congratulate them.

10   LinkedIn blog post is liked; this is a great way to connect and amplify their content.

11   LinkedIn blog post is shared, see 10 above.

12   Comment on your blog post; this is a great way to engage

The problem with listening is, of course, that the sheer volume of information on social and digital networks can be overwhelming, and this makes the job difficult. There are almost 100,000 tweets, 100 LinkedIn accounts and 1,500 new blog posts created every minute.

To quote Clay Shirky (in his 2008 Web 2.0 Expo talk), the problem is not information overload, it is 'failure to filter'.

Buying signals are occurring all day, but you can't spend your whole day listening (you have other work to do if you are to close that sale or retain that customer!).

Listening should be frequent but brief. This can be facilitated by using the right tools, which will cut through the white noise and can be built into your working rhythm to minimize the time you invest. In Chapter 8 we discuss some of the tools that can help you listen to customers, prospects and competitors.

What is your own brand DNA online?

If you want to own your territory do not make the mistake of thinking that all tweeting is good and any content is better than no content. Wrong.

As discussed above 'you are what you tweet' and people visiting your LinkedIn page or Twitter page will make a judgment on you from that. People who are boring, over-tweeting corporate suits will be passed by.

Think what it is you stand for. What is your personal brand DNA? You need to start making judgments about what you tweet. Does it meet that standard?

For example, I avoid anything that I wouldn't want to discuss with my granny, so I avoid politics, religion, anything rude – pretty much anything that might cause offence. I'm not saying don't post it; you might be running a Twitter account for the next president of the United States. But if you are posting articles that might offend your customers, guess what? When they find you, they will be offended, so don't. Open up another Twitter account for anything controversial.

Understanding what you stand for is critical. I was helping a guy that sells Human Capital Management (HCM) software, and he was in a tailspin about all the content he could share. We sat down, had a one-to-one and talked about what it was he would stand for. He decided that the subject that interested himself most was work/life balance. This he decided was to be an area where he would 'own the narrative'. He would find all the articles on this and write some too. After a discussion on hashtags he put on 200 followers in a week, just by people being able to find him and find him interesting.

How do you find content?

Nowadays there are some amazing 'content curation' tools. They do all the hard work in finding articles for you. Products like Flipboard, Pocket, Medium and Bundle Post all have algorithms that will search for articles based on the criteria you put in them. For example, you can get articles on the subjects you want to be famous for; filing cabinets or work/life balance, etc. We mention a number of these tools in Chapter 8 on technology.

Once you have those articles, you need to filter through them. Which ones meet your own brand DNA, which will your followers find interesting? Are there articles that might enable you to grow your following?

Hashtags

One of the ways to get found across all social networks is the use of hashtags. When Twitter first started up, the only way you could search on data was using hashtags. It has since changed that you can now search on any data (we often use Twitter to search for information rather than Google). Hashtags have now entered into day-to-day language, so much so that every brand will have a hashtag. I've seen organizations create mission statements, backed up with hashtags.

If you want to be found then you need to use hashtags that your customers are using to search for information. While some of this is trial and error, you can start to search for terms for your niche on Twitter to see what you get.

For example, I once tweeted 'The 10 best places in the world to buy chocolate' and then added the hashtags #food and #drink. If people were searching for articles on chocolate then it would be picked up as that word appeared in the tweet. But if people were searching on subject matter related to it then a nice summary would be #food. Therefore, people searching for food-related articles would also pick up that tweet.

Hashtags are used a lot on Instagram; in fact they are now used there more than on Twitter. They don't tend to be used on LinkedIn as people are searching for people and companies rather than content, although with the driver of more and more blogging on LinkedIn this may well change.

In a recent training course we gave to a large B2B enterprise company, one of the attendees had 600 followers but had flatlined there for months. Looking at his Twitter feed, which was informative and interesting, it was clear (to us) why the follower growth had stopped. Nobody could find him.

After 30 minutes learning about hashtags, he put on 200 followers in a week and last time I spoke to him he was accelerating past 1,200 followers.

Twitter lists

As your Twitter following and the people you follow grows, I highly recommend that you start using Twitter lists otherwise you can soon waste time and effort. You need to get organized.

Lists are a way to start grouping subject matter areas or people into certain sections.

The best way to think about Twitter lists is that they are similar to a library. How do you find a book in a library? If you want to find a book on fly fishing then you go to the sports section and in there will be a subsection on fly fishing.

With Twitter lists you can collect similar companies or people around certain subject matter areas. For example, Big Data, Cloud, Filing Cabinets, Desks; all the people or companies that talk on those subject areas. You might want to have lists on your customers or competition. You are able to fine-tune the subject areas.

You can also subscribe to other people's lists; for example trade shows and conferences will often have lists of attendees or people using the conference hashtag. Why not jump in and engage and retweet with these conferences? I've been itemized on leader boards at conferences that I haven't even attended, but they were in the niche I worked in and just by being interesting, I've picked up followers.

You can also use lists to group maybe your favourite sports teams, news channels or any interests you have.

Then when you have that spare 20 minutes in your day, go through one of these lists and see if there is anything your following would be interested in, and if so retweet that. If there are articles you want to read later then like those. You can go back to them later on.

You don't need to spend hours on this, but 20 minutes a day is an excellent time to invest in growing your personal brand.

It is often at this point in my training sessions that people ask me about automation. As one person said to me, 'Why don't we just automate this, we can go back to doing our day jobs'.

In Chapter 8 we discuss the pros and cons of automation and how it can help, but also hinder. Social selling is social. People expect to be able to engage with you. Your Twitter and LinkedIn feed belong to you, and they reflect you out there in the digital world. Many people think that automation 'saves time'; it's all about how many tweets you can get out there. I'm sorry but if you use tools to post and have no time to engage, people will immediately recognize you as a robot/bot, soon lose interest and unfollow. (Don't forget people can unfollow just as quickly as they can follow.)

The 4-1-1 rule

Many people ask me what rules I follow when I tweet, or how I know what to tweet. My advice is to follow your gut instinct and tweet what you think is interesting and will help your buyers, followers and community.

The 4-1-1 rule for Twitter was popularized by Tippingpoint Labs and Joe Pulizzi, founder of Junta42 and the Content Marketing Institute (the earliest use I can find is from 2011).

The rule states that:

> You share four pieces of relevant content written by others, one
> self-serving (about your company product or services) tweet and one
> tweet that shows you as a human being. Such as your football team, you
> walking the dog etc.

What's great about this approach is that it lets you engage in the conversation, build awareness, and keep in touch with your followers without coming across as pushy or too 'me' focused.

The 4-1-1 rule can also apply to your lead nurturing using LinkedIn. Formally, lead nurturing is the process of building a relationship with prospects that are not yet sales-ready by conducting an informative dialogue, regardless of budget, authority, or timing. Less formally, lead nurturing is the art of maintaining permission to 'keep in touch' with potential customers as they educate themselves, with the goal of being top of mind when they are ready to move into a buying phase.

This is where the 4-1-1 rule can apply. As you plan out the cadence of LinkedIn posts, try scheduling four educational or entertaining posts mixed with one 'soft promotion' (eg attend an event) and one 'hard promotion' (eg download a free trial or apply for an account).

Online and offline community

With the move to social, there has been a creation of both online and offline communities. In the earlier chapters we discussed how creating a community or tribe was a requirement of a modern day salesperson. That said, social is a channel; you don't stop talking with people or engaging with people offline.

Social is a way to listen to the market, find the people and nurture them through stages until they 'pop' into the offline funnel or as some sales leaders say to me, 'the normal funnel'.

The other things that sales leaders say to me is, 'All this personal branding is "interesting", but where are the leads?'

The leads are all in this community at the top of the funnel for you to find. Personal branding, listening and using signals are all ways that you will find the leads, or better still they will find you.

Social selling best practice

All good sales professionals research their target accounts (no different than we have done for the last 30 years) but now we can do this online. During this research we can listen to an organization, business issues, or news items. We can also research and listen to executives to target Twitter, LinkedIn or even Instagram. Wherever our customers are, we need to be.

Just as when you go to a meeting with somebody and they have photos on the wall of their office, so too can you find out about them if they are posting on Instagram. People often ask me, is this snooping? No. If people are posting photos publicly then in fact they want you to find them and engage with them.

One way you can engage as a social seller with your target accounts is to engage with comments such as, 'Noticed you were talking about XYZ; have you considered this?' 'This' being some content that the contact will be interested in to drive the conversation forward.

A friend of mine looked for signals to contact one C-level person, and tweeted to him, 'Great to see this technology being rolled out'. The executive replied and they got into a dialogue. My friend told the executive he had a presentation that might be of interest, so the executive then followed Paul back so they could have a direct message (DM) conversation. My friend shared the presentation.

With some good research and a degree of luck, you should get a follow back and then enter into a DM conversation. A direct message conversation is private, and as such can be used to directly identify leads, or as a precursor to that.

You are not limited to 'salesperson to prospect' conversations; standard DM (or Twitter room) functionality allows you to add pre-sales or support people to bring in a specialist domain skill.

Foursquare and Swarm let you 'check in' to locations, using the geo-location functionality of your phone. Thus you can see where your prospect currently is. If your prospect is posting this publicly, why not use it as a way to say, 'I'm in the area, or just down the road, why don't we have a quick 30 minute get together?'

Word Swag is an app that we use that allows you to create quotes against a pictorial background. This type of personalized micro content is getting a high-level response rate. Get inspiration for a Word Swag from listening and researching your target across social media. Then send them the Word Swag as part of a tongue-in-cheek engagement.

In summary, use Twitter and LinkedIn to research your customers and prospects, both at a company level and for the actual people you need to connect with. LinkedIn say that for every enterprise sale, 5.4 people are involved in the decision-making process, so you need to go deep and wide. Use LinkedIn and Twitter standard functionality to suggest additional people, or people connected to those people (they may well be connected in person and influence).

Listen to what your customers, competition and prospects are saying. Use Google Alerts, Hootsuite, LinkedIn Sales Navigator, Google+, Twitter, Facebook, Instagram and LinkedIn as ways to do this. Don't forget that LinkedIn only accounts for 30 per cent of your social graph, and it won't show up family relationships; this will be uncovered on Facebook. The CEO you are calling on may be the sister-in-law of a colleague. It would be a pity to miss that 'base' just because you use Facebook for family and friends.

Engage / share. Use the usual platforms such as Twitter, Facebook and LinkedIn. But you also should spread your sharing to Instagram, YouTube and SlideShare. SlideShare and YouTube are great places used by B2B and B2C buyers for (detailed) research into new products and services. Follow people, look at their profiles, like, retweet or comment on what your prospects, customers or influencers are doing.

Connect. It is at this point you should use LinkedIn InMails (best practice shows a 7 per cent acceptance rate; that's a 93 per cent rejection rate). Send tweets or use something like a Word Swag. There is nothing wrong with you making contact via e-mail or calling them as the relationship should be 'warm' (rather than cold) and you are not interrupting, but offering help/knowledge/value.

Nurture. Have you ever contacted somebody and they have said, 'All very interesting, but give me a call back in three months'. At least you are now on their radar. You can then nurture the relationship. You can do this through a marketing automation tool. You can also do this through LinkedIn. Connect with them and then the articles you post will allow you to nurture them. This won't stop you calling them in three months, but if for any reason a project kicks off before then, they should know where you are; you may be the first person they call.

Summary

In this chapter we have taken you through the behaviours that you need to exhibit in the new digital world. You need to create a personal brand online, so what is it that you will stand for? What is your own personal brand DNA? What subject matter will you tweet on? How often do you need to tweet and importantly, how can you be found when you tweet?

Everybody, including your customers, is leaving 'footprints' on social media, and these are all signals that you can interrupt to engage and help your prospects or customers. We have itemized a number of signals as examples. Different signals require different tactics. But don't forget, this isn't about diving in and selling. This is about helping and teaching. Selling can come later in the buyer journey.

We then finished with some good social selling practice, or how not to be a spammer. Educate and inform your reader when you are on social, make them curious for more. Better still, get your reader to make a 'next action' to connect with you.

Bonus material

The following bonus supporting resources are available at **www.koganpage.com/socialselling** (please scroll to the bottom of the web page and complete the form to access these).

- How to use hashtag guerrilla marketing.
- Employee advocacy programmes.

Selling the idea of social selling and measuring success

07

Sales leaders say to me that this personal branding stuff is all very well, but where are the leads?

In this chapter we go through the common objections you will get to running a social selling programme, and how you go about getting sponsorship and with whom. Plus we look at how to measure such a project; the difference between different metrics.

At the start of the book we explained how the 'internet had changed everything'. Our customers now use the internet and social channels to research and buy goods and services. In order to undertake social prospecting, companies need to be on the channels where their customers are active. Social prospecting will give us the leads, and using the sales techniques that we have built up and continually craft we should be able to close these leads ahead of the competition, giving us the revenue at the margins we want.

In the book we talk about how to create community and use influence to control our markets. Community should not be seen here as a hippy concept, but a tool that can be used for competitive advantage.

The opportunity

A piece of research that has been quoted so many times throughout the industry it is now considered fact, states that buyers spend 65 per cent of their time online. With its original source long since lost, official 2015 buyer statistics by the UK Government Office for National Statistics (ONS) go a long way to support this:

- Sixty-nine per cent of 55–64-year-olds bought online in 2015 (45 per cent in 2008).

- Both men and women have increased their internet purchasing throughout the period, with the percentage of men purchasing online having increased from 57 per cent in 2008 to 77 per cent in 2015 whilst the percentage of women purchasing online increased from 49 per cent in 2008 to 75 per cent in 2015.

- More men than women buy goods and services online, but the gap is narrowing.

(For a direct link to this research, see our References list at the end of this book.)

Once the buyer has undertaken their research they will usually come up with a shortlist of two or three vendors. The buyer of today is well informed and well researched, and by the time they have created a shortlist they understand each short vender's value proposition as well as price.

If as an organization you have invested and implemented the techniques in this book and find and engage these buyers early on then your competition will be lower and there will be little price friction. If you decide not to change to the sales techniques of the digital world then you will be left to fight over what is left with all the other suppliers, creating most likely the need to drive your margins down. In addition, research shows that the online buyer tends to choose brands as a shortlist.

If, for example, you are a small- to medium-size organization, you are most likely to miss out, as these buyers will shortlist the bigger brands. But the good news is that small and large companies alike can use the methodology outlined in this book. That said, communities and owning the influence in your market can be obtained with little need to invest in big and expensive tools.

Common objections and how you get around them

'My customers are not on social...'

This myth is an interesting one. This goes back to salespeople talking about companies as if they are a single entity. I'm sorry, but I cannot believe that in the company you are selling to, 100 per cent of the employees don't use social. Even if you think that your customers are totally offline, what about your prospective customers? Your competition? There is a whole world out there that wants to connect and you are going to pull up the drawbridge and sit in your analogue castle?

Don't forget that social media requires a relatively low investment, but if used in line with the methodology in this book, it can have a high impact.

Your audience is freely telling you about themselves on their online profiles. You can use their social profiles to learn about their personal interests and what topics they wish to discuss. You can use this to target and engage with them.

Why would you shy away from creating an expert reputation for your business, the go-to point for everything that your company sells, creating an online monopoly that wins deals, creates revenue and maintains good margins?

People that just don't 'get it' or don't want to

Presentation skills courses will often say that when you present, cast your eyes round the room and look to see who is engaged, who is falling asleep, etc. As we tour the world talking about how to make a change to the selling process one thing I notice is that often I see people's eyes glaze over.

While this could be because of my presentation skills, we often have the chance during question and answer sessions or networking to seek these people out (be warned!) and ask for feedback. Once a person said to me, 'All this talk about social networks, sorry I have just no idea, I'm not on Twitter and have the minimum on LinkedIn. In fact you have got me thinking that I cannot wait for my retirement to come around.'

We are certainly not being ageist here, as 'social blindness' infiltrates through all ages, cultures and backgrounds. However, we have moved into a digital age, and therefore people and businesses must move with this change if they want to remain competitive.

In many cases we've seen senior management give salespeople prizes for the number of followers they have, or the number of tweets they have made in the last time period. This for me is really scary, as it's clear that the management don't understand social.

Of course it goes without saying that we always research a company's senior executives and the people within the company before meeting them. We then make a judgment (as do so many other people, potential customers, potential employees, your competition) on your organization based on your social profiles.

It's not just sales and marketing that is impacted here but the war on talent and the experience your customers have when interacting with you.

We guess that by reading this book you already did 'get it', and even if not, by now you must have come to realize that the 'battle' for customers and market leadership has moved online and you need to be part of it. Or you might do what many companies have done, which is delegate it to a younger age group (although it is worth saying that I'm not suggesting you turn over your social policy to teenagers...). Our recommendation is to look for people in the organization that are young enough to understand social, but also have the business acumen to support the advice they give you.

We also recommend that if you have bosses or staff that don't 'get it', you simply buy them a copy of this book and give it out as a present. We have had sales and marketing leaders that have given this book en masse to their staff.

This social stuff is all 'fluff' – just go and get me leads and revenue!

We hear this from all the sales leaders, and vice presidents that we work with. All this stuff on personal branding and using social media is kind of interesting but what they want are leads, which convert into revenue (at good margin).

In fact, when we first pitched this book to the publishers, Kogan Page, they said to us that they didn't want a book on personal branding; their feedback to us was 'there are enough personal branding books in the world'.

The objective instead has been to give you a platform to use social, but use it as a tool that will drive your leads (preferably inbound) and while we don't say that you need to stop cold calling, social should be used alongside this as a channel to cultivate prospects and customers.

It's worth breaking off from social for a moment to talk about cold calling. We have all been in the situation where we have that deadline to meet and we are creating a PowerPoint presentation or Excel spreadsheet for that all-important board meeting. We have scoped it all out and we have pent-up creativity that we just need to get out of our heads and into the computer. We are part-way through this amazing streak of creativity when the phone goes.

We all know this will probably be a cold call and for most people we just ignore it. (Sorry, salespeople reading, we know you will ring back.) If we do take the call then we know that the telesales agent will probably have a well-crafted script to take us through in order to get a yes. This just frustrates and annoys us and just makes us feel animosity towards that company, the opposite of wanting to buy. By then we are so wound up that by the time we get back to our board presentation, we have forgotten what we were going to write.

Yes we agree that 'interruption' cold calling is dead. As a sales guy said to me recently, 'I've just spent the whole day cold calling and got nowhere, surely there has to be a better way?'

The mistake I've often seen people make is they say they are 'totally moving to social!' There are many social selling gurus out there that say that cold calling is dead; I'm sorry but it isn't. It has evolved, and used with the techniques mentioned in this book along with tools such as marketing automation, it is alive and well and creating many a meeting.

How to position social selling with your executive team

Social selling is a strategy that must be driven from the top. That's not to say that without C-level buy-in you needn't bother, but without it you will bounce along with what I call 'random acts of social'. See Chapter 9 on the Digital Maturity Model.

To get buy-in you can (and we would recommend it) run a pilot. We take a bunch of volunteers (people who volunteer are usually partly social and early adopters). We then take them on a three-month journey to turn them into social sellers, offering a measurable journey (agreed with the management), so we can see that it is results-based. Finally we present the results and conclusions to the board.

We usually find at this point that one of the senior management will volunteer, and we work with them to help them become social so they can understand the journey we are proposing. Don't forget that 'one size does not fit all' and that different leaders have different motivations; you need to work with them around these drivers.

For example, marketers will maybe have more interest in brands, as well as leads. Sales will be interested in leads as well as using social through lead progression and closing. Don't forget that personal branding, employee advocacy and talent management can all have a social impact and that the human resources department may well be affected.

In the next part of the book, we look at the different department heads and how you should position your pitch for a social selling project.

Chief Executive Officer (CEO)

When we talk with CEOs these are the usual concerns that they raise:

- How do they grow revenue, while maintaining margin?
- How do they attract and retain the best talent?

- How do they innovate and out-execute the competition, and what is the plan to still be around in five years' time?

- How to enhance collaboration in the organization, and break down those silos!

So how to position social selling with CEOs?

- Contextualize social selling as the key to top-line growth. Supply statistics about how social selling is connected to revenue, and position it as the future of the modern sales organization. Offer to run a pilot, which will have an agreed set of metrics.

- Highlight how social selling will separate you from your competition. Show how your competitors are relying on the old sales playbook, and contrast your competitors' efforts with your plan. Social selling will give you a competitive edge and enable you to control your influence and 'own' the markets you trade in.

- Talk about the performance improvements that you'll gain from knowing exactly which selling tactics are working and which content items are resonating with your buyers. I've seen efficiency gains of 25 per cent on the workforce by using collaboration technology; that's the equivalent of 25 per cent more people at little or no cost.

Chief Finance Officer (CFO)

The CFO, in most cases, is the person who 'writes the cheques'; often you need to convince them even when everybody else is in agreement.

We find the main concerns of CFOs are:

- Managing expenses: build a business case and show an ROI within 12 months, starting with a pilot phase to prove out the initial expenditure.

- Containing risk: explain where things can go wrong (change management etc) and show how you will manage it.

- Planning for the future – once the return on the investment has been obtained, what then? Show how you can drive revenue (and margin) growth.

How to connect the dots for the CFO:

- Present your developed business case. You must always have a business case when talking with a CFO. We recommend you get an independent third party to 'cast their eye' over it, as the CFO will often go straight for the numbers and the detail.

- Use benchmark statistics to project how social selling will affect revenue. Your CFO will understand if you have to use estimates; simply note where you are using them.

Social selling requires building relationships, communities and influencers, and educating buyers, both of which take time. Therefore we have to change the way we think about the costs associated with social sales.

In short, social selling is an investment. Your company incurs costs today, but social selling delivers benefits for many months and years to come. By investing in training, technology, and pipeline today, you're setting your team up for success in the future. We come back to the pilot to show that while this is long term, there are 'quick wins' you can implement to show a return in the short term.

It's like buying a house. The returns from buying a house are not immediate. They often come years down the road – when you go to sell your house. The same is true of social selling. Over time, when you have moved to being a digital organization and your sales and marketing are online your investment in social sales will pay off.

Head of Sales

Salespeople and sales leaders will always be thinking about the following things:

- How do they hit or exceed quota? Sales is a numbers game. How will you get a continuous stream of meetings to close? If the leadership think social is all about 'kids posting photos of lunch' then you need to explain how you can connect the investment to 'the numbers'.

- How do they get an accurate sales forecast, which they can publish?

- Create references so that customers buy more or tell others to buy. Many want a lower cost and repeatable sales process, especially in the new world of SaaS (software as a service).

- No sales leader likes being beaten by the competition.

So here's how you sell them the idea of social selling:

- Remind sales leaders that buyers are deleting e-mails and ignoring phone calls. By using social networks, creating communities and online knowledge champions your sales teams will stand a fighting chance of engaging their buyers.

- Show how social selling is a way to beat your competition. By reaching out to buyers before they approach your company, your sales team can start shaping buyers' attitudes early on, and in turn, your reps will win more deals.

- Highlight the ways in which technology will help you standardize best practices across your sales team, by using modern best practices such as lead nurturing. These free up salespeople to spend more time in front of clients.

- Use this book, the statistics and research reports available to you. Highlight the fact that buyers use social media when making purchasing decisions. Remind people what they do when they want to buy something. They don't dive in and ring a supplier; they go online and research first.

- Note that sales teams are more likely to attain their sales quota when they use social media. But this isn't about chasing vanity measures such as likes and followers; it's about using it as a tool to find new prospects. You can still measure people on meetings, revenue, or whatever metric you currently use. This is NOT about 'playing on Facebook all day', which is a common objection we hear.

Chief Marketing Officer (CMO)

Here's what a CMO wants to do:

- Strengthen relationships with customers; it is easier to sell to an existing one than a new one. Plus, how can we work with the existing customer base to get new customers – isn't 'word of mouth' always the strongest sales tool?

- Build alignment with the sales department. It is important that the two departments don't 'throw stones at each other', but work together with a common goal and purpose.

- Measure and prove marketing ROI. This we have seen time after time – how can we prove that the leads we created were actually due to our marketing efforts? Are we measuring the customer journey or the last touch?

- Protect brand equity. With customers buying (or remembering) experiences, how can we make sure that we create and protect the brand and its DNA?

And here are a few tips for connecting the dots:

- Put social sales into context. Identify ways that the marketing team has evolved over the years through marketing automation, content marketing, moving the marketing budget online and other initiatives. Then, position social selling as a way of modernizing the sales organization. We often see social selling initiatives start in marketing (as it's seen as a lead generation tool) and then flounder as the sales department only see and hear 'fluff' rather than actual revenue. Don't forget people will want you to 'show me the money'.

- Discuss social selling as an opportunity to bring marketing and sales into better alignment. For example, the programme will empower the salespeople to generate their own leads, reducing pressure on marketing. It gives marketing activities greater visibility in sales so you don't get the 'you never tell us about your events' situation. Also by bringing sales and marketing closer, there is a greater understanding of what a lead is, so we move away from the thinking that 'marketing-created leads are rubbish'. Trust me, this can take effort, change management and constant dialogue; we have seen sales leaders and CMOs start sending each other Christmas cards.

- Assure the CMO that the company's brand will be protected. Highlight your plans for social media training, and indicate that marketing can supply content and sample messages to the sales team. Sales reps won't be on their own. The big mistake that companies make is thinking that LinkedIn, Twitter etc can be used just like Google and Amazon. No – we have never seen a 'How to use Amazon' training course, but setting up LinkedIn and Twitter to drive leads and revenue is different. It needs training (one to many) as well as, often, one-to-one coaching. You might say, well we would say this, we run a training and coaching company, but we have been in so many meetings where people say they 'get it' and they don't. People are frightened of admitting they don't understand social. One-to-one coaching will enable us to focus in on the particular issues somebody may have. For example, one person we coached put lots of effort into social but flatlined at 400 followers on Twitter (a common problem). Just by sitting with the guy for 30 minutes we enabled him to put on 200 followers in a week. How? He had been tweeting but nobody could find him, so with just a little coaching on how to use hashtags and a bit of guerrilla marketing and he was away. Within a month he hit 1,000 followers.

- Explain that social selling will not compete with marketing's social media strategy. Social media marketing speaks to large segments of buyers, while social selling offers an opportunity for personalized 1:1 interactions. Most of the marketing departments we talk to understand the difference and want other employees to help. Often they find they need help but don't know how to go about asking for it.

- Emphasize the idea that social selling will amplify marketing's efforts. Sales will rely on marketing's content to build relationships and check in with customers. Without paying for advertising, more people will see your company's marketing assets. Creating a community will amplify the brand messages and get them to areas where marketing probably didn't have the resources to ever reach.

Getting a budget approved is infinitely easier when you have buy-in from other departments. Sometimes, your buy-in is literal, in that other departments will contribute monetary funds. Other times, your buy-in is simply support for an initiative. By getting the marketing and human resources (including training) departments involved, you increase the size of the budget.

Chief Information Officer (CIO)

It's not often we talk with CIOs but when we do, these are their chief concerns:

- Controlling costs; they will want to make sure this isn't a back doorway for another IT purchase.

- Innovating and evolving infrastructure for the future. Many IT departments suffer from legacy systems that use 80 per cent of the budget just to support them. IT resource is tight; CIOs don't want their staff distracted.

- Managing technology security, so that it meets the company's cyber and hacking policies.

- Most CIOs now understand that they must make investments that support the company's goals.

We find the following useful when working with the IT department:

- Paint a picture of the future. Show how sales teams need software beyond the CRM. They need mobile and social media tools as well. Life isn't just about adding the names and addresses into a CRM system; people need the social context. What is a person's network? Who are they connected to and who do they influence?

- Get buy-in from your marketing team, as well as sales and maybe even the HCM department. CIOs are more willing to approve technology if several departments are interested in it.

- Get the CIO to understand that Twitter and LinkedIn are 'standard' social tools.

Getting buy-in for social selling is not always easy. But if you understand your stakeholders' concerns and position social sales accordingly, you have a good chance of convincing your executive team. Don't forget we are also available to help.

Return on investment (ROI) and criteria for success

To get approval for new projects, you need to establish criteria for success. In this part of the chapter we will talk about these. Some of these measures we admit can be seen as 'fluffy' but we will explain why they can help. We will talk about the hard measures that will make a real monetary impact on the business.

Since social selling is an investment, it may take time for your programme to pay off; as mentioned above, even with a pilot you should still be looking at an ROI within 12 months or less.

Revenue metrics may not be the best indicator of success in the short term, but these measures can show if you are on the right or wrong track. If a piece of content gets 10 likes, so what? No, this does not have a revenue impact, but it does mean that 10 people liked it (which is good, yes?) and you got distribution and amplification of the content over other people's networks (which is good, yes?)

For this reason, to start, you may want to focus on engagement metrics. Think about numbers related to the amount of content shared, clicks, reach, and network growth. These are early signs that your tactics are working and that your team is on its way to building relationships and driving revenue.

Different types of metrics

When it comes to social selling programmes, businesses can measure their progress in several ways. Below, you'll find three types of metrics. Choose the metrics that make the most sense for your objectives, your role, and the maturity of your programme.

Training metrics

It's easy to get ahead of ourselves when it comes to launching a programme. We want to start as soon as possible, and we forget to take the time to build our foundation. It is too easy for employees (and it's usually the 'non-believers') to skip training, and this means that it will take you longer to show success. You will also get 'random acts of social' which are often off-putting to those who are struggling with the concept.

Training should be a key part of any social selling programme. Unless you train your team, you will never meet your programme and revenue objectives.

Here are several ways that you can measure training:

- average number of training hours;
- average time to competence;
- percentage of employees who are certified;
- number of training sessions held for employees;
- percentage of employees above competence;
- percentage of employees below competence.

We always recommend a certification process, as this means you know that the team has at least reached a baseline. This certification process, delivered by the management, shows that there is leadership buy-in. Otherwise, like any change programme, people will go back to their old behaviours.

Tactical metrics (they may be 'fluffy' but they do show momentum)

Another way to measure your social media efforts is through tactical metrics. To state the obvious, these measurements help you determine if your tactics are working, if your content is liked or disliked, and if you are gaining the growth and amplification you need across your communities and networks.

Are your salespeople's posts engaging their followers? Are people clicking on their tweets? Are they retweeting your content?

Many of these metrics are useful for your curators – the people who have to write compelling messages for your sales team. These numbers will help your curators optimize your programme going forward.

Here are different tactical metrics that you can use for the three major social networks.

LinkedIn

- *Number of posts per day.* We would expect a salesperson to manage at least one.

- *Number of connections.* Any enterprise salesperson should have at least 500 connections and at least 50 per cent of these should be across their community of accounts, contacts, influencers etc.

- *Number of comments, likes and shares.* Salespeople should 'share the love' and like and comment on at least one (each) post per day. We live in LinkedIn; it is open all the time we are working. Unlike maybe Facebook where you can get distracted with cat photos, with LinkedIn you should be working 100 per cent of the time.

As we discussed earlier, getting your content amplified across people's networks is good. Don't fall into the trap of only being connected to mates and work colleagues; grow and nurture your network on LinkedIn. If you have potential clients then maybe they will pick up on your content (and even make contact with you), when they start their research.

Twitter

- *Number of posts per day.* Salespeople should be posting (and engaging) at least once a day.

- *Number of followers.* Salespeople need to have upwards of 400.

- *Number of @ mentions.* Salespeople should get one a day, and share the love by mentioning other people at least once a day. This is social media after all.

- *Number of retweets*. Salespeople need to be interesting enough, with a big enough network, to be RTed at least once a day. They should also be engaging enough to RT themselves once a day. And please, not to just your mates, as you will end up talking to yourself. Salespeople need to know how, by using hashtags, they can get their content noticed by their audience.

- *Number of lists each salesperson is listed in*. Salespeople should want to own their territory, offline and online, and should want to be picked up on lists so their content is amplified.

- *Reach*. How many people saw your post? Salespeople need to get their material out to not just existing customers but to people who haven't even thought about their goods or services yet.

Facebook

Please don't think Facebook is for 'friends and family'; LinkedIn only represents around 30 per cent of your social graph. There can be relationships on Facebook, for example brothers-in-law etc, that don't show up on LinkedIn. You might call upon a CEO who didn't show up as having any connection with you when you researched them on LinkedIn. If you had looked on Facebook you would have found out that they are your brother-in-law's best mate. They play golf together. Certainly an important fact to know when you go to such a meeting. Yes?

While the measures are pretty similar to LinkedIn and Twitter, our advice is NOT to post the same article to every network. Facebook contacts will prefer non-work-orientated posts, softer subjects. You can be a thought leader, but leave the suit off and be more 'jeans and t-shirt'.

- *Number of posts per day*. At least one, but no more than two or you start looking like a spammer.

- *Number of friends*. You need to be pushing 200. Yes it's OK not to be friends with your boss.

- *Number of likes*. Jump in and engage.

- *Number of shares*. This is a 'super like', people will still see posts that you have liked.

- *Number of comments*. Engage with people and don't forget, as posts are pretty much public, to be a beacon of niceness. Our advice is to not post anything that might offend your grandma, and like with friends (or you lose them) keep away from politics, religion, smut and profanity.

A few words of advice

1 *Number of posts*. The number of posts per day will vary by network. On LinkedIn and Facebook, you want to post between once and twice each day. On Twitter, you can post between 10 and 12 times per day without annoying your followers. DO NOT batch up posts and 'spray' them out to all networks via automation. This is NOT a time saver, you will lose followers quickly.

2 *Number of comments*. Some people will comment on articles just to comment on articles. Other people will comment only if they are prompted by a question or a specific call to action – something along the lines of, 'Let me know what you think'. If you are seeking commentary, play around with different ways of soliciting remarks.

3 *Number of link clicks*. If you are trying to get people to read your content, there are many factors to consider, such as your article's headline, whether you included a picture, whether you included a shortened link, where that link appeared in the post, the type of content and the social network that your content appeared on.

Experiment with different factors and figure out what works best for your audience.

Sales funnel metrics

With sales funnel metrics, you're trying to see how your programme influences your sales funnel. For example, are you generating new leads? More pipeline? More revenue?

Sales funnel metrics are focused on money. These are the types of results that executives care about. But funnel metrics should not be the only numbers you analyse. Without a strong strategy and guidance to build communities that will pay, you'll never be able to influence your sales funnel.

Here's a short list of some of the sales funnel metrics you can analyse:

- Number of new leads and meetings generated from your social selling team. Maybe use a campaign code in your CRM for leads created through social.

- Number of social media touches with leads, pipeline and customers; where is your website inbound coming from? Can the sales team get inbound from LinkedIn and Twitter?

- $ of pipeline generated from social selling activities; are the sales team driving and generating leads via the use of social?

- $ of revenue generated from social selling activities; are they using social for lead progression, de-risking deals and competitive strategies? Are they using social to help close deals?

- The average contract value of your deals generated from social selling; can you increase your deal size (ability to cross sell) with the use of social?

- Sales cycle; the average amount of time that it takes for your social selling team to close a deal. Can you reduce the time it takes to sell?

Words of advice

1 **Social sellers vs. non-social sellers.** If you have a large sales team, you may want to run a pilot before you roll out a social selling programme to the entire sales organization. Compare the sales funnel metrics for the salespeople who are using social media to those who are not. See, for example, if your social media team has a shorter sales cycle than your traditional team.

2 **Be realistic.** There isn't a magic silver bullet in the sales world. If your current sales cycle is six months, don't expect to

suddenly close deals in one week simply because you launched a new programme.

3 **Be patient.** It's going to take your team some time to adjust to their new sales mentality. Being helpful and building relationships take time. It's much easier to deliver cold pitches and hope for the best. But in the end, your patience and hard work will pay off, and you will generate more revenue. We recommend continual coaching sessions, so that you can fine tune the behaviours. Some people will pick this up and 'fly', but others will need support. It should be possible to build self-help groups within your organization, but then again, don't distract salespeople from what they are good at: being in front of customers. Social should aid, not hinder that.

Final words on metrics

We looked at one small facet of a social selling programme: metrics. What you measure will depend on:

- your role;
- your programme's maturity;
- whether HR teams will care about training metrics;
- whether curators and social media managers will be concerned with tactical metrics;
- whether your executive sponsor will be interested in sales funnel metrics.

In addition, the maturity of your programme will be an important factor. How long has your programme been running?

New social selling teams with long sales cycles may not see revenue growth for a few months. So, looking at revenue may not be the wisest move straight away. Instead, you may want to look at pipeline growth first, or you may want to focus on standardizing tactics across your team.

Bear in mind that, while metrics are an extremely important component of any social selling programme, they are not the only component. All sales programmes involve many moving parts.

After the pilot

Once you have completed your pilot there will be lessons learnt (given that all sales teams are made up of different individuals). There will be things that worked and things that didn't work. An open and honest feedback process should work out best practice and then work on rolling that out across the organization.

The best people to do this are salespeople themselves. Our role has often been to organize and support, and the best way to sell the programme is to have the initial pilot group saying, 'I closed this big deal because of social, and you would be a fool not to do it'.

Pan-European projects

While I know some readers may be in small enterprises, for those in large pan-European or pan-global organizations, our recommendation is to run pilot projects in-country. With a project such as this that can have change implications and localized differences, a UK-centric or US-centric view of the world should not be imposed on other countries where the culture and use of social may be different.

Finally, some questions you should be asking yourself

- What are the goals for social selling?
- Why should your sales team care?
- How used to change is your organization?
- Have you defined your target market personas?
- Could there be multiple personas? You may, for example, sell accounting systems, but there are many different people in finance you need to sell to. LinkedIn estimates that for every enterprise deal, 5.4 people are involved.
- What is the timeline in which you want to see a return?
- How does your company use social today? Is it integral to marketing?

- How does the sales team currently use social?
- Have you rolled out any social selling schemes to date?
- Has there been any training to date?
- What has worked to date? What has not?
- Do you have the resources to create your own content?
- Have any metrics been placed on the sales team for social?
- How does the sales team use content currently?
- Is there a culture (be honest) of building trust with clients online?

Summary

In this chapter we have taken you through the different ways you need to sell a social selling project internally. How for each decision maker and persona you need to make a different case. Our mantra throughout the whole of this book is to try to keep the measure based around how many leads you will create and therefore how much revenue. The temptation is to get sidetracked with vanity metrics.

Bonus material

The following bonus supporting resources are available at **www. koganpage.com/socialselling** (please scroll to the bottom of the web page and complete the form to access these).

- Why sales and marketing departments need to work together for a common purpose.
- How do we measure the customer journey?
- Advice on how to run pan-European projects.

How to use technology to your advantage

08

One of the most common things we are asked when we are being interviewed or when on the speaker circuit is what tools do we use. This chapter is a round-up of the tools we use as well as some tools which we know other people use to good effect.

We have placed this chapter later in the book so that you the reader will have by now bought into the idea of a social selling strategy; the need for owning and dominating your community by listening, contacting and engaging with people, influencers and competitors alike. It is only when you own the online world that you will enable yourself to gain a market-leading position.

You do this by engaging, adding value and educating, but not by the old 'analogue' rules of sales muscle, large advertising budgets and big discounts. In the new 'digital' age, anybody with little budget (but time) can build a world-beating business that can own and dominate their community.

Jill Rowley says, 'A fool with a tool is still a fool'. In the next chapter on digital maturity we talk about 'random acts of social'. This is where some people in a department will start using a tool, but have no connection with the strategy.

Tools will save you time, free you to do other things and bring more and better engagement. Tools also allow you to collaborate with other departments – sales and marketing working together for example. But if they are used outside of the context of the overall strategy then these are just random acts of social.

We have broken the tools you can use down into four areas:

1 **Research** – How can you use social networks as a way to find things out, such as your next targets for a marketing campaign?

2 **Automation and scheduling** – How can you post into your news streams to your niche and community to educate or evoke engagement? You want to do this outside your normal posting hours, for example.

3 **Content curation** – How can you find materials (written by somebody else) that you can post in your social network news streams that will be interesting to your niche and community?

4 **Content creation** – If there is not the content then how can you create content that will attract people to your social networks and website etc?

Research

Talking to strangers – discovering more about people

In Chapter 3, we talked about the need to grow your network and own the community you work in. This means you need to talk to strangers. We mentioned how you don't just walk into a room and shout at the top of your voice, 'Hi, it's Tim, we have 30 per cent off this week', as many brands still do in the offline world. If you go to a networking meeting of, say, 100 people, it may be that only five are useful to you as a social seller. How do you find out before that meeting which five people you really need to talk to? We then explained in Chapter 3 about how you then go and listen to what they say, before joining in with the conversation.

There are a number of tools that allow you to do your homework and check people out before you go to a meeting. What are their passions? Did you go to the same college? Are there people you trust that you share in common? What is it that will turn that 'cold' conversation to a warm one?

Connect6 – Connect6.com

Connect6 is a free Google Chrome browser plug-in which gives you a social snapshot. When you are browsing Twitter you see a small beacon next to the person's details. Hover over this and you will be able to see the person's other social networks. You can see a personal connect path and also get contact information. The same goes for Gmail, where you can see people's e-mail social connections. This is a great way to check if something is spam.

The paid version of Connect6 is a database of people's social details (550 million at the time of writing). This is particularly interesting to people who don't want to use a scattergun approach but want to get a narrow focus of contacts. For example, if you are a start-up seeking funding then there will be only a few investors that might be interested and you can focus down and make contact with them; alternatively you might be a recruiter or in financial services and have a particular financial product to sell.

At a networking event, there are only some people who will be interesting to you and this enables you to find them. It's a bit like in the old gold rush days, where people had to pan for gold; here you can get those 'nuggets' quicker and easier.

Crystal – crystalknows.com

Crystal is complementary to Connect6. Once you have found the people you want to connect with, Crystal has an algorithm that works out the best way to communicate with them.

The algorithm looks at people's profiles and then makes a judgment on their personality and the best way to communicate when you make contact.

Couple this with a good understanding of somebody and this can be very powerful, especially if you are like me, and don't like rejection. With the success rate of a LinkedIn InMail being 7 per cent, which is a 93 per cent rejection rate, Crystal will increase your likelihood of success.

Sidekick from Hubspot – getsidekick.com

Sidekick is a Google Chrome browser plug-in that allows you to track e-mails you have sent. This allows you to see who has opened your e-mail, if they have forward it internally etc, enabling you to prioritize the people you call back.

With all these tools, they are often free but require you to pay to get more functionality. Sidekick allows you to see mutual connections you may have to the people you are e-mailing, which will help you with a warm introduction.

FollowerWonk – moz.com/followerwonk

While I don't use this tool, I've had it highly recommended to me. While there is a free version, you need to expect to pay money if you want to get real value from it.

It enables you to build your community by searching Twitter bios for those target personas and allows you to search their contacts, networks and communities. This will enable you to find their influencers.

You can analyse your followers by location, bio and who they follow, and contrast these relationships with your friends and competitors. By reviewing unfollows you can see what tweets people like and dislike, which enables you to fine-tune your content strategy. You can also follow and unfollow people.

Analysing your content

When you are taking the time and effort to post created content, is it the right content? There are a number of tools you can use to measure the response. In our experience measuring what is good or bad content based on an unfollow is a pretty inaccurate science. People may be annoyed beforehand and just unfollow for the sake of it.

When building a community, you have to be mindful of your content, especially if you are trying to make an impact on key influencers or pick up on subjects that people are talking about, to raise your share of voice.

In the projects we have worked on, we have listened to what people were talking about, then decided on what topics would resonate with the community and personas we wished to market to and influence.

We decided that we would go along with two subject areas people talked about and the third we would build from scratch and in effect create our own market place.

Tools that automate and schedule

The way to build community is to have high-quality content to educate, but it is also to engage. When somebody said to me, 'Why didn't we automate social media and go back to doing our day jobs?' they were missing the point. One of the first subjects we get asked about as soon as somebody masters how to use Twitter and LinkedIn is how to use automation. The question usually arises as they don't really see they have time for social media, so they want to automate it and... you guessed it, go back to doing their day job. They then wonder why they don't progress very far after 150 followers. They are being boring online. Why would anybody want to follow them?

This is where people totally miss the point. Social media and using social for your work is not about banging out content and hoping somebody will pick up on it, OR banging out more content than the competition, often called 'share of voice'. Content is there to help buyers; offering people an endless 'fire hose' of noise won't get you more leads or more sales.

If we go back to that drinks party, does anybody like the person talking only about themselves and their work? No. So why do it online?

Automation does have its place as it frees you up to do other things. If, for example, you are running a conference, you can use automation to send tweets about the day. 'In 10 minutes', Tim Hughes will be talking about Social Selling, in room 2B'; you can automate that. This frees you up to engage with people tweeting the content from the conference.

If This Then That (IFTTT) – ifttt.com

IFTTT is an application based on the idea that 'if this happens, then it will do that'. It comes with standard 'recipes' that other people will have written, that you can then use. These recipes do not need any programming experience; you just pick the ones you want in the app and connect the systems.

For example, whenever I accept a connection on LinkedIn, this is automatically added to a spreadsheet in Google. Whenever the weather looks like rain, I get a text from weather.com reminding me to take an umbrella, which is useful in London.

It also allows you to get round certain 'issues'. For example, Instagram gives you the option to post a photo to other social networks. If you post to Twitter, Instagram posts the text and a link to Instagram, completely losing the impact of the photo. By using IFTTT, you can post your photos from Instagram to Twitter and you can see the photo in full.

The use of IFTTT is limitless as more and more brands build out functionality. For example, there is an iPhone application that will switch the lights on when it detects movement. This can be used for burglar detection or deterrence.

You can also track work hours into a Google calendar, save the photos you have taken to Dropbox, send photos from Instagram to Flickr, etc.

Clearing your profiles

Tweepi – tweepi.com

In terms of social selling, Tweepi allows you to find users that might be interested in your brand. Once you have found them you can 'interact' by following or adding them to a list. By doing this your targets might just come and have a look at your profile and better still they might follow you back. This increases your reach and amplification.

This is an app I use to manage my Twitter accounts. It allows me to see which accounts are not following me back, and which accounts have unfollowed me (I unfollow them). It also allows you to 'spring clean' your Twitter account. For example, you can unfollow inactive accounts (by number of days), users that don't have a photo, bio-less users, and followers who are inactive. This enables you to have a pretty spammer-free Twitter environment.

Discover.ly – discover.ly

We interviewed the CEO of discover.ly for our blog, and they have a great story behind how the Google Chrome plug-in was created.

In previous chapters we have talked about social graph, a term that Facebook came up with, which describes your social network. Of course, as we use different social networks, our social graph is in silos. We recommend the use of LinkedIn, but it is only 30 per cent of the social graph.

Many people say to us that Facebook isn't for B2B sales, and that they just use it for family and friends.

Ted, the CEO of http://discover.ly/ used to be the product manager for the Salesforce.com Chatter product. A salesforce.com sales guy called upon a CEO of a company, but what that salesperson didn't know was that CEO was a relation of Ted's. There was no connection on LinkedIn showing that the CEO and Ted were relatives, but there was on Facebook.

Discover.ly allows you to see people's other social networks as you surf LinkedIn, and it also shows you their last four tweets as well as insight into their Gmail network. This is all interesting if you are calling on a CEO and want to get some background information or points that you might have in common.

Hootsuite – Hootsuite.com

Hootsuite and Buffer are tools that allow you to automate your social posts.

Hootsuite also allows you to listen to hashtags or certain words, and to schedule posts in the future.

Hootsuite has always seemed to me a great tool if you wish to have an editorial schedule over a few months or few weeks and need to create these tweets in advance.

This has advantages; as we mentioned earlier it can free you up to do other things or allow you to post them outside of your normal time zones. For example, 55 per cent of my followers are in the United States and I might want to post something I want that market to hear or amplify. Also, if you are running a conference or have a campaign with a whole stack of tweets, then maybe this is the tool for you. Be sure though, as we mentioned earlier, that you don't just walk away from the tweets but make time to converse with anybody that engages. After all, it is the engagement that will bring you the leads and meetings.

The disadvantages are that tweets can be set up ready to happen but then something happens to disrupt it. There have been situations with supermarkets where there was an issue that hit the news and then the tweets that were automated suddenly became highly inappropriate, causing the main news item to blow up even more.

Buffer – buffer.com

We are big users of Buffer. The free version of Buffer allows you to 'buffer up' eight tweets in advance. In a usual day, I will buffer up eight tweets in the morning and then another eight tweets in the evening to pick up different time zones.

That said, I always build in time to go through all the day's engagement and comment, thank and take comments, maybe with direct mails (DMs). It is usually this that offers 'inbound' requests for work. Don't forget with any level of automation to find time for engagement. In B2C, customers now expect a one-hour response time. In B2B we still see that a response time of eight hours seems OK.

Riffle and Nimble – crowdriff.com/riffle and nimble.com

Riffle and Nimble are both Google Chrome plug-ins that allow you to check people out ahead of a meeting. If you look somebody up on Twitter, it shows the other social networks they appear on.

Riffle by CrowdRiff teaches you about a prospect's social community. It's a good way to learn about your prospects to enable you to 'break the ice'. It also gives you the top five people they interact with, which enables you to build out your network.

Nimble is another Google Chrome browser plug-in that allows you to investigate people before a meeting so you can try to find areas of mutual understanding or contacts. Nimble can stand alone or work with the Nimble CRM system. I often tell the story of a call I had with Jon Ferrara, the CEO of Nimble. As mentioned earlier, Jon lives in California and his time zone is eight hours behind mine. Normally when you get on a call with California from the UK the first things you discuss are what the time is and what the weather is like. On this call, Jon opened up with a question. What was my favourite vinyl record of all time?

What he had done was take the time to investigate the fact I collect vinyl records, so the first 15 minutes of the call consisted of a discussion of our best gigs and bands we had seen. What a great way to start a sales call, building rapport.

Content curation

As part of your Twitter and LinkedIn news feeds you will need to post articles or information that will create curiosity in the reader (who is hopefully your next prospective customer) and they will respond or get in touch with you. Or they might think, this is an interesting person, when I next need those services I will get in touch. Either way, the way you work in the online world is not to put out this week's offer but to provoke thought and educate. In the B2C world, many brands are engaging with customers and hopefully prospective customers by using humour. The gambling sites are a good example of this.

The 4-1-1 rule

The mistake we see many people make today is using social as a way to push out as much content as they can. Often corporations have content creation teams and they see the employees as channels to push out that content. Employees are often given no training as to why or how to share, and will just do what they are told.

This is where the 4-1-1 rule comes in. We are not saying follow this rule religiously, but when you are first starting out it is a useful rule of thumb.

The rule is this:

4 – Post four items of information you have created that you think will be interesting or should educate your audience about your niche area. The key thing is these are NOT written by your in-house team.

1 – Post an item that is corporate or is written by your in-house team.

1 – Post something that is funny or is personal to you. It might be a cat photo, a photo of your dog when you take them for a walk, a photo you took on holiday. Either way this post is designed to humanize your Twitter feed.

Note: on LinkedIn all of the posts should be serious in nature, so we suggest you leave the final 1, cat photos, dog photos etc, off LinkedIn.

Which apps are available for content curation?

We use apps such as Flipboard and Medium as places to find content, more so on Medium as this is also an application that allows you to create your own content.

Flipboard comes with a number of standard magazines that you can follow, and you can also set up your own search words. For example, if one of your key terms is 'big data' you can use Flipboard to pull together all of the articles on this app which use that term. This then gives you a wealth of articles that you can decide to post through your various social networks.

In addition, as you have a readership that is hungry for content, you can then create your own magazines that people can follow and consume that content. Hopefully the outcome will be that readers will amplify the articles through their own social networks.

Some brands have tried to 'stuff' Flipboard with corporate articles, but because they are obvious sales brochures in disguise they don't get shared and often the brands give up as they don't get the followers or shares. Some brands have been successful at putting out educational material that has been shared. At the end of the day, the fact that an educational article has appeared on a brand's blog is enough to trigger the association or the 'like' for that brand. You do not need to be sales-y in the digital world.

Content creation

We highly recommend that salespeople start creating their own content. In the digital world they cannot rely on 'marketing' to create the content that will create the initial curiosity that a prospective buyer might have when starting down a road of research. In addition, we highly recommend that a salesperson creates a personal brand and will want to own their community ahead of all the other salespeople.

If, for example, you are selling supply chain systems into the process-manufacturing sector, surely you want to own that market? Be the person that people turn to or the opinion that is valued? In the past this was 'simple'; you called up your territory and found the people that might have been looking at that moment. In the B2B world this is usually about 5 per cent of the market. In addition there will be another 25 per cent that will say, 'Interesting, but call me back in three or six months'. How can you do deals with these? More on that in a bit. But how can you cover that 70 per cent of the market that has maybe never thought about your products or services, or may be just about to start out looking.

By being a thought leader, as a salesperson in the market you are in, it is highly likely that people will seek out your opinion, even if you work for a brand. It's better still if you are seen as an 'influencer'.

In the digital world, 'anybody' can become an influencer. With the right community, content and open attitude they can be a 'beacon' that attracts people hungry for knowledge and wanting to be educated. It is with that knowledge and education that they can go back to respected companies and start procurements. Hopefully you will be on the shortlist OR maybe you have used your analogue sales skills and already closed the contacts.

Content creation platforms

There are three main platforms for you to create or place content.

1. LinkedIn

Many people are turning to LinkedIn as a place to put out content; usually this is in short form – about 500 words, so a single page of A4. This is a great place to get a subject matter out quickly and as it is published in LinkedIn it will go out to your network and hopefully your network will share it to their networks, etc.

LinkedIn is a platform (due partly to books like this) where people are very hungry for content and your blog should get shared pretty quickly and extensively. This will enable you to grow your community and following.

Tips for LinkedIn blogging

The headline and initial photo are everything. For people to find you and be intrigued enough to read and then share, you must give this a lot of thought. Somebody once sent a blog for me to read which had a three-word title offering no reason for me to think I should read it. When I gave him feedback, his response was, 'Yes, but surely when somebody had read it, they would get the title'. He was correct, but I doubt anybody would read it.

The first sentence is the 'hook' that will drive the reader to read on.

My advice is to write no more than 500 words. Some people do write more than that, but I'm not sure if it all actually gets read.

As I write, LinkedIn is making the leap into mobile with its own Pulse blogging platform, which should be a hit with LinkedIn users.

2. Medium

Medium has been created from the ground up as a blogging platform to be read on mobile, which is probably where many of your future readers will consume your content. Again this is often short-form blogs of 500 words, but many people put out blogs that can be 1,000 words or more.

This is another platform used by people who are hungry for content and the blogs are made easy to share on social networks, giving you amplification.

Medium allows you to follow people and to be followed; if you are followed then people are told by Medium when you blog.

3. Wordpress

I've used Wordpress for two years, as I wanted to have my own blog. Wordpress present to the novice a number of templates (many are free, some you have to pay for) with a quick start in terms of the overall look of the blog. Wordpress say that they power 25 per cent of the World Wide Web. I cannot verify those figures but many small companies use a Wordpress blog as their first website.

While LinkedIn does provide some statistics for your blogs and numbers of shares, Wordpress provides you with extensive statistics, such as where the traffic is coming from and then where it goes.

This is important as you can focus on where you want to drive the traffic from, such as Google, Blogger platforms such as Medium, or social networks. Wordpress will show you if a person who visited your site then undertook a next action. When you are building a community one of the best ways to get a next action is to get the person to sign up to your e-mail list. This is critical, as they are then told when you blog. We are lucky that when we blog many people share our material, which increases our amplification.

We highly recommend that if you use Wordpress you get into a cadence of publishing articles at the same time on the same day, regardless of the pressures to do otherwise. Why? This is good for Google and your Google rankings.

Google has what they call spiders that go out and look for content to be ranked on their site and they are always looking for new content that shows engagement. If you are putting out content at regular intervals, sometimes the spiders might actually be waiting for you to publish.

Getting somebody to sign up to your e-mail list

Getting somebody to sign up to your e-mail list is difficult. Why would somebody put their e-mail at risk of you spamming it? What we recommend is to offer a long-form eBook to people who sign up. This is about the size of a book chapter, 5,000 words, and offers something educational that they cannot get anywhere else.

So by offering this value, people are getting something and are more likely to give something, for example their e-mail.

Does your content resonate with the market or what influencers are saying?

Buzzsumo and Onalytica – buzzsumo.com and onalytica.com

Both have tools that allow you to 'pour' in your content. They will analyse it to see if people and influencers are talking about those subjects, and you can then make a judgment before publishing as to whether that content will resonate.

We have worked with a number of companies where we have tested different versions of white papers to test for their market resonance before publishing.

Measuring influence and amplification

This book isn't about the details of these measures; we just want to point out that they are there and do have their uses. I've often used measures as a way to see if I'm doing the right thing. If my Klout score has moved from 45 to 50 and my LinkedIn SSI has moved from 55 to 60 them I must have the right behaviours.

Klout

Klout is a measure of social influence; love it or hate it, Klout has created a narrative where people discuss the pros and cons of their 'Klout score'.

This book isn't about whether Klout (or Kred) is good or bad, but it allows you to measure the relative 'influence' of a person, assuming that a high Klout score is influential.

I'm aware of people who scam Klout by using automation. So while they had a high Klout score there was no amplification of their message, so they were in effect posting and nobody was listening. A high Klout score, for what?

Klout allows you to measure your influence across many platforms such as LinkedIn, Twitter, Instagram, etc.

We have often seen it being used during the 'random acts of social' phase where somebody with some knowledge of social in an organization thinks it would be a great measure to use. When people are starting out, it isn't. Why? When somebody is starting out on social, they need to focus, find their voice and get comfortable with life online. This is unlikely to move the needle much with Klout.

For example, to get a high Klout score you need to post a number of times a day, and this usually requires automation. You need to open your Facebook right up so the posts are public and you probably need upwards of 250 friends. For people who think that Facebook is for family and friends, this just isn't for them.

LinkedIn SSI (Social Selling Index)

LinkedIn recently produced the SSI, which is based on your usage of LinkedIn only. We have run a number of workshops for companies where we have used SSI as the starter measure, really as a way to get people comfortable to start posting, getting a buyer-centric profile, starting to like and share. For a beginner this is ample.

Finding influencers

In Chapter 1 on building a community we talked about influence and how you find it. You can find influencers by just being 'out there' on social; you are always welcome to drop by and say hi to us. Twitter and LinkedIn are good places to find influencers.

On Twitter, find some time to look at the news feeds of people you trust; they will I'm sure tweet or retweet articles from their influencers. Then when you find those influencers, you can find who influences the influencers, etc.

You will often see lists produced from time to time that are usual places to find people of influence, but they come with a health warning. There is a well-known story of a person who wanted a job at an organization, so he created a list with people from that organization in the top 10. Just be careful, as often lists are created for an agenda.

Two tools for finding influencers

We are aware of and have used these tools for finding influencers; they are both tools you need to pay for.

Traackr and Onalytica – app.traackr.com and onalytica.com

Traackr is a French software house that allows you to find influencers to help build your community. We have used both this and Onalytica to good effect.

As you grow your network and community you need to find the right influencers that can impact your business and your buyer's decision-making process. This may be the 'usual suspects' but also you may find people like ourselves who have influence but are not multinational companies.

As you build your influencer network, you will need to gain insights on your influencers and plan initiatives that will let you work together. It was suggested to us once that influencer marketing was easy. Find the influencer and then send a salesperson off with a white paper under their arm to make contact with them.

We had to challenge this. You have to remember that influencers are just that. What happens if they tweet, 'I've just had some idiot from XYZ Company come to see me with some boring white paper'? That's a PR disaster and then all your competitors know what you are up to.

You must have an influencer programme (a programme is a project with no end) and develop focused, value-add relationships with your influencers. Use metrics to prioritize outreach, measure the impact of your engagement and report on the efficacy of your efforts.

Traackr is a cloud-based product, whereas Onalytica is a product that provides a service.

It's worth stating at this point that when searching for influencers they may be both online and offline. Don't forget to find and nurture the offline ones. Often you will find that journalists are still very offline. For example, they will have some online presence but their channel is really still newspapers and magazines. They still have influence, so don't just stick with the tools online and think that's it.

Other tools

Instagram

While we have not talked much about Instagram, it is worth getting into, as it is a great place to post photos. In addition, it is a useful place to do research on your prospects and customers. For example, people may post photos about dog walking or fly fishing, etc.

We use the free version of Instrack to track our Instagram followers, discover who has unfollowed us and who is not following us back. You are also able to detect users, view your fans, and rank your best friends. We are not massive users of Instagram but the engagement is excellent and you do find B2B brands on there. Also, if you are doing research on people and companies, it can often help fill in gaps.

Word Swag

Word Swag is an app that many use that allows you to create quotes against a pictorial background (see below). This type of personalized micro content is getting many social sellers a 90 per cent response rate, which is only a 10 per cent rejection rate. Compare this to LinkedIn InMails, which give 7 per cent acceptance and 93 per cent rejection.

For example, social sellers will research a senior influencer, but in some cases might not be able to track them down on e-mail or the phone. Having researched them on LinkedIn and Instagram, they can create a Word Swag as a different way of making an approach.

Do your research, create a Word Swag and increase the likelihood of getting a response.

FIGURE 8.1 Example of presenting a tweet using Word Swag

WE HAVE NOW REACHED
A TIPPING POINT WHERE EMPLOYERS HAVE
A DUTY OF CARE TO THEIR SALESPEOPLE TO IMPLEMENT
A SOCIAL SELLING PROGRAMME!
-@TIMOTHY_HUGHES

Foursquare and Swarm

Foursquare and Swarm let you 'check in' to locations using the geo-location functionality of your phone. Thus you can see where your prospect currently is.

When I did some training on cold calling the advice was to move the discussion away from a decision on a meeting – yes or no – to an option. The advice was also to pose a question such as, 'Can we get together to discuss this? I'm in the area next Tuesday or Thursday, which is better?' This moves the emphasis away from a yes or no decision to the meeting, making the dilemma over when to meet, Tuesday or Thursday.

Social sellers can use this in a number of situations where they are able to say, 'I'm in the area, or just down the road, why don't we have a quick 30 minute get together?'

You can also use IFTTT to 'double dip' the information so you can get traction/engagement on LinkedIn, for example, as well as Swarm. We are aware of social sellers getting a meeting with a marketing director where he had posted on Swarm but the post was picked up (via IFTTT) on LinkedIn. As many big brands are now 'listening' to social media, the fact that somebody is checking in with them means (based on your well-crafted message) they may want to engage as much as you do.

I'm aware of people who have had free coffees, but that isn't the real reason why you are reading this book, I'm sure.

Summary

In this chapter we have taken you through the applications we are using today to help us in our social selling endeavours.

Due to the nature of technology advancing so quickly, it's worth noting that these platforms are likely to move in and out of use, but the intention of the chapter is to show the theory of how these concepts increase sales, advance opportunities and complement each other efficiently from different perspectives, rather than how to use these platforms specifically.

Digital maturity

09

Companies will have different digital strategies and these will be impacted by how mature they are digitally. It is not always the case, but in our experience the digital maturity of an organization is connected to the digital maturity of the leadership.

From the outset of this book we have said that social selling is a strategy that requires top-down support and leadership.

That said, to quote the visionary management consultant and author Peter Drucker, 'Culture eats strategy for breakfast'. The argument goes something like this: strategy is on paper whereas culture determines how things get done. Anyone can come up with a fancy strategy, but it's much harder to build a winning culture. Moreover, a brilliant strategy without a great culture is 'all bark and no bite', while a company with a winning culture can succeed even if its strategy is mediocre. Plus, it's much easier to change strategy than culture. The argument's inevitable conclusion is that strategy is interesting but you need culture.

We can propose a strategy but this has to be driven from the C-suite, by C-level people who understand why they need to move from an analogue to a digital sales and marketing way of doing business.

This is where we get the 'I get it' syndrome.

Many C-level people we meet were top of the class at school and college and nothing has beaten them to date. When we get asked to talk about social at board level, there is a lot of nodding and comments like, 'I get it', but we actually find that, 'I get it' means, 'I don't get it, but cannot admit it in front of the other people in the team'. The forward-thinking nature of these people leads them to believe that as they have mastered everything else in life, surely they should get social. Which is why we are often pulled in to offer them one-to-one coaching sessions.

Social media is all about trust

A common objection we see at a leadership level in organizations is that 'social is for kids'. Many leaders see their children using social and think that is the only way it can be used, posting photos of lunch.

The most common question we get when we present is, 'Is there an ROI in social?' We then talk about our friend who is getting 10 C-level meetings a week by using Twitter. He has been creating ROI for two or three years now by 'messing about' on Twitter and LinkedIn, which is why we have discussed using real digital sales techniques, using community, and direct revenue-generating measures from social as key drivers for such projects.

So where does trust come into this? Well actually it is about companies exerting control. First we saw companies banning access to social media; now they want employees to use it but in a way that is controlled by the corporation.

Sorry, but once the 'genie is out of the bottle' it cannot be put back in. More people are getting social every day, including our customers and competitors, and corporations must give employees the freedom (and this means they must trust them) to go onto social media. Just think of the free advertising your company would get if you allowed your employees to talk passionately about working for you, the pride they have in your products and services, and how they like to serve and excite your customers.

This passion will be infectious, it will help existing buyers to buy more, it will pull, like a magnet, customers over from your (boring) analogue competitors, and it will attract the best talent. You are then in a virtuous circle. The more passion within your organization, and the better talent and competitors' customers you attract, the more revenue and margin you make.

Or let's let things play out the way they do for your boring analogue competitors. In the 1980s when I started to work, we had a typing pool. For those too young to know what that is, you scribbled out the letters on paper and handed them to the typing pool, where they would type them up for you. We then moved into the world of word processors, AmiPro and Microsoft Word, where the numbers of letters you could pump out increased. Then with the invention of e-mail, you could pump out an infinite number of them at 'zero' cost.

The maths of this is simple. To increase your return on investment, you increase the number of e-mails you pump out. It's all based on the law of averages. We know the average percentage click-through rate, so we know how many e-mail addresses to buy. As people click on e-mails less and less, you have to buy more and more e-mail addresses. Where do you think this all ends?

In today's customer-led market, the sustainable advantage is in knowledge and engagement with customers; owning the community, listening and engaging with customers and influencers and locking the competition out. The quality of your customer experience will unlock that in the digital/online world, where your customers are.

It's worth noting that customers work and transact across different channels. If we stop to think about our own buying journeys, we might research something on mobile (YouTube, blogs) on the train to work, and then when we get to work we might look at a website and have a live chat session. Brands must offer these channels to customers seamlessly; you should not miss out on a customer touch point along that journey or you will be left behind.

In the path to digital, there is a clear dividing line between digitally mature and digitally immature.

Digitally mature companies are looking to transform their business with a clear digital strategy supported by leaders who foster a culture to change and invent the new. Meanwhile the digitally immature are focused on discrete business problems, mainly throwing technology at them and hoping it will stick.

The digitally mature understand that they have to take people along with any change programme, and this will mean training or retraining. The digitally immature will let people 'self-serve'. We often see they have a view that if nobody went on an Amazon course, why would you need to train people on LinkedIn or Twitter? (Until somebody makes a PR mistake and the 'shutters come down'.) This is the Talent Challenge.

We are often introduced to the digital team, and we know we are in trouble if we do our research before that meeting and find they have little or no social presence. We are not saying that everybody has to be a thought leader but being put forward as a digital expert when you have 150 followers on Twitter or no social presence does raise some questions.

The view from boards in digitally immature companies is often that social presence can be purchased, like on the TV programme X-Factor. Press a button and you have 100,000 followers. As one senior manager once said to me, 'Why don't we just automate social media, then we can go back to doing our day jobs'.

We explain that being social is more Bob Dylan than X-Factor. Putting in time 'playing to folk clubs with an audience of seven people' is a great way to find your voice and know instinctively what tweets and hashtags work to excite your audience and generate a next action.

Social selling maturity

So far, we have discussed how social selling is the way to sell in the digital world and while you don't need to throw away all analogue process (such as cold calling) you do need to start the journey to move your work ethic and that of your company to the digital way of working.

As we have mentioned this requires engagement with social selling both at a strategy level, and within the culture of your organization.

FIGURE 9.1 Social Selling Maturity Model

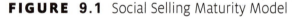

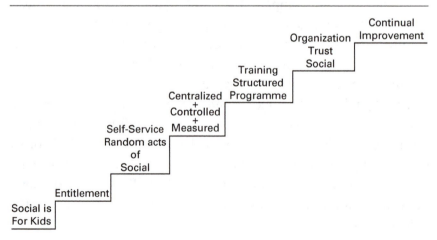

How to implement a social selling change programme

Making the change over to digital selling will not happen overnight. You cannot just 'flick a switch', putting training courses on the intranet or even hiring a trainer.

Social selling requires sales professionals to change the way they do business every day. Changing behaviour is the biggest challenge that sales leaders face.

This social selling maturity model has been developed based on experience of social selling projects – what has gone right and also what has gone wrong. It would be great to try to get in at the top, but sometimes you have to learn and make mistakes to reach the greater goal at the end.

For example, if you have children, most people have the goal to give them life experiences and make them more rounded. One step in their development might be to climb a tree. We all know they are highly likely to fall; some will bounce, others will break an arm. But we have to be there for them and sometimes the broken arm is part of their long-term development.

Stage 0 – Social's for kids

We get pulled into many organizations where well-meaning people, usually at 'shop floor' level want us to sell the idea to management that they have got to get social. We usually find that the management has no social presence and end up presenting to a bunch of people with folded arms and glazed eyes.

The best way to approach this situation is by having a group of salespeople forming a pilot to show the ROI.

Stage 1 – Entitlement

At this stage, somebody has probably read about social selling in an inflight magazine or attended a conference, and a project is kicked off. Often it is kicked off in marketing, as there is this belief that digital selling is all about demand generation and not about the total sales process. Modern marketing has a whole bunch of terminology that companies have to get used to: MQLs (Marketing Qualified Leads), BQL (Business Qualified Leads) etc. This is great, as it means that now when we describe a lead, we are all talking about the same thing. We will talk about marketing automation in a bit.

Stage 2 – Random acts of social

At this stage the management may run a programme or even tell the employees to be social sellers. Maybe standard LinkedIn courses are offered on the intranet. Little or no guidance is offered. Individuals create accounts on social sites such as LinkedIn and Twitter.

There is a complete lack of coordination (management are usually allowed to get away without being social). The early adopters drive activity, but there is no organizational governance, coordination or risk management.

With little or no education and training, we often see these programmes fizzle out; they are seen as yet another management fad and people go back to doing what they did before.

Digital selling is supposed to bring sales and marketing together. Some people call that 'Smarketing' others call it 'Smales', and at this stage it can often add to the cross-departmental 'stone throwing'.

Marketing often have responsibility for demand generation, and as the social selling article on LinkedIn that the senior manager read was probably written by a marketer it will all be about demand generation.

As a senior manager recently said to me, 'There is no ROI in social selling, we tried it in marketing and it didn't work'. It was difficult remaining polite and not saying, 'Social selling, the clue is in the name'.

Often with random acts of social, you will find they duplicate, and confuse or even just isolate people. If people don't understand social, throwing buzzwords and jargon at them won't help. I once saw a campaign run by a guy using Klout scores, and people asked me, 'What is Klout?' This is classic; it just isn't relevant when you only want people to grow in confidence in social.

From an overall standpoint the impact of social selling at this level is limited without a formal programme in place. At this level, the organization will be selling the greater percentage of business through analogue methods and the narrative will be analogue. You will get some uplift of sales through social, but it won't be transformational.

Stage 3 – Control

People use social every day; it is omnipresent. With random acts of social spreading through the organization and the number of Twitter accounts proliferating, things can often get out of hand. There is often a PR disaster. How long before somebody has a bad day and tweets something negative?

Don't forget PR is a highly controlled process. Companies only publish the message they want people to hear. PR in many companies is still the 'denial' method. PR managers just deny that anything is happening, and it becomes the job of journalists, through clever questioning, to get that 'quote' to make the headline.

The response to that from companies is to offer 'media' training to employees. Only registered 'spokespeople' are allowed to talk to the media.

Now anybody can say what they like.

There are also sites like Glassdoor, where employees and former employees anonymously review companies and their management.

For somebody trying to control a message this is the stuff of nightmares. You mean, anybody can post anything? Yes! Then they need to be shut down.

You may recall from history at school the story of King Canute and the waves. To flatter him his courtiers told him that he was so wise and powerful that he could even stop the tide coming in. The story goes that King Canute was not so gullible and told his courtiers to take him to a beach whereupon he would command the incoming tide to go back. Of course, Canute demonstrated he had no control over the elements (the incoming tide), and that 'trying to stop the tide' was futile. There is the PR department's dilemma.

What usually happens at this point is that the potential risks are realized and people step in to bring discipline and consistency to the company's branding and messaging on social networks.

This stage is useful as often there is a realization that social selling will happen. The companies then write and distribute a social media policy. They establish a process to monitor employee use of social.

I've seen 'outlier' figures that have created their own social brand in Steps 0 and 1, and are in fact often the social leaders of the future; they either come into conflict with the organization or get shut down. Many have left, often poached by the competition, who are a step further ahead in maturity. Organizations need to be looking for these individuals, working with them and nurturing such talent, as they will be the ones driving the digital selling programmes forward in the future.

It is also worth noting that often policy and process are imposed without training and this often confuses. People have said to me, 'I stopped posting, as the rules allowing me to post are so tight, I don't bother anymore'. This defensive position has little direct benefit for sales performance, and is often described as 'taking one step forward and two steps back'.

Stage 4 – Structured programme

Having established a marketing, legal and compliance foundation, companies are now in a position to empower their sales team with a structured programme. This will take the form of training, but does not mean that the management are on board or 'walking the walk'.

The training at this stage usually takes the form of LinkedIn training in the belief (as with many social selling 'gurus') that digital selling equals LinkedIn. As we mentioned previously, LinkedIn is only 30 per cent of your social graph, so the salespeople miss the opportunity to build and own strong communities.

The training often revisits the programmes introduced before, which is really a personal branding project, enabling the company to pump out as much company content as they can. This is often hidden under a banner of 'share of voice'. That is, can we compete with all our competitors, in an 'arms race' to see how much content we can pump out?

This comes back to the history of 'pile them high' marketing we talked about earlier. First we pumped out letters, then e-mails, and now we pump out content; in all cases we crossed our fingers and hoped it would stick. Hopefully, having read this book, you will see this isn't how you run a modern marketing and sales organization.

If the training covers more than personal branding and also looks at how to talk to strangers (etiquette for making new contacts), social prospecting, content sharing, content creation and community building, then such a programme should start 'moving the needle'.

During the programme, the leadership must signal their desire, perhaps an expectation, that salespeople need to use networks to sell. Marketing must provide sales with content that is vetted and approved to post and share. It is probably very 'corporate', which is why salespeople need to think about creating their own content, but that won't happen until we get to trust.

Note: it is pointless creating content unless you measure its success. We talked in the previous chapter about how we can use metrics such as likes to measure impact, and there are tools that can help with this. For example, you can find out how long people actually watch your YouTube videos.

Despite many benefits, impact achieved in the training stage is limited by two factors: measurement and scalability. Managers cannot measure (easily) how employees are or aren't acting on the information communicated in the training. And training is difficult to scale, especially where there is high staff turnover. Sales teams overcome these limitations when organizations move beyond one-off training and when social is woven into the fabric of the organization.

Stage 5 – Trust

A social selling programme will not blossom until an organization places trust in its employees. I'm not saying that you can accelerate straight to this place; most often, as with any change programme, this is a journey people need to make.

Trust is the opposite of control and organizations will want to control the uncontrollable. It is only when they have wasted many hours and dollars trying to push the genie back in the bottle that maybe they will realize that it cannot and will not happen.

There is only so far you can go with empowering people and yes, progress can be made, but it is only when management trust employees that the full potential is achieved.

There must be many of you reading this who are saying, 'This will never happen in my organization', and I agree, this may well be the case. We usually find that it requires a major catalyst to make it happen, such as a change in leadership, usually (but not exclusively) to a 'younger', social-savvy person. Or where the CEO is driving a company-wide digital transformation agenda. I am aware of a very large organization where it is working, but it took the recruiting of a (not so young) very charismatic leader to push it through.

So why trust?

Organizations have to let go and trust people and the passion they have for their work. Sorry, but if you're not passionate, maybe you should go and do something else.

We live in a society where we make purchase decisions about products on Amazon through reviews from people we have never met. We make decisions on hotels via TripAdvisor through reviews from people we have never met. Often the fact that a person is a friend of a good friend makes their recommendations alright for us. People no longer read ads; they would rather speak to somebody in their network who has used a product. This means that ordinary people can influence purchase decisions.

But – and it's a big but – companies who are controlling when it comes to social for employees just don't get it. The first thing you think when an employee says how great their company is is, 'Of course they would say that, they are biased, as they work there'.

This book isn't about social media, it's about social business. If you look at how business worked in much of the 20th century, it was based on the production line. Everybody had one. It was what you did with it, how you treated the people and the raw materials, that gave you competitive advantage.

In the world today, it is not what you know, but what you share with the communities that you build. When you have a company that is sharing knowledge internally and externally then you truly have a 'game changing' situation. And there is the difficulty – how can you trust people to share knowledge outside the company and not give away all your trade secrets? How can you share to attract and retain customers and talent?

Don't forget, you are already paying your employees, and if they like where they work and are passionate about the company, then they can become even more valuable for your marketing programme.

Of course, not every employee will want to assume this role, but giving those who have a passion for your company and product an outlet on public platforms such as social media can drive even more loyal and engaged employees. We are seeing that socially native people see blogging, tweeting and updating LinkedIn and Facebook as things they do every day. Many of us have moved our lives online and it is natural for us to live and work there.

From our own experiences, when customers can experience happy and engaged employees, either in person or on social media, this leads to happier and more engaged customers. Who doesn't want to buy from a company where the employees are proud of where they work and happy to say this publicly?

So why not trust your employees to talk about the company? OK, you can offer guidelines and have disclaimers but you cannot ignore their passion. But you can ignore boring corporately written tweets and posts.

Companies have to start with the recruitment process. You will find your digital workforce online. Every time these people tweet something, they don't even need to mention their employer, as people already know they work there. Maybe it's digital product placement.

Every time your trusted employees tweet something it's listened to. This is a win-win situation. It's a win for your employees' personal brand and a win for the enterprise as they get an authentic voice and not just press releases being regurgitated. Don't forget you pay these people already, so you don't have to turn to outside influencers.

There are already companies whose employees are intertwined with their customers on social, or customers that have left the organizations you are selling to but still have an influence on that company through their network. It is very possible you need to call upon company B to sell to company A, as there is a previous employee of A working at B.

So where are these people? Often they already work for your company, and you just need the leadership to harness and trust them. If you had your employees passionately talking about your company, this would give you such a massive lift. If you also pull people into a community you can create an unstoppable force. Or at least move yourself to a market leading position.

In summary, a smart brand advocate programme can help turn employees into advocates, and happier, engaged employees can translate into developing loyal customers who become social advocates as a result.

Stage 6 – Continual improvement

At this stage social is embedded in everything that you do. It's not an "add on" but people are living and breathing it. At this stage there should be a culture of trialling new developments and apps and dropping or adopting them as required.

Optimization

We have stated many times in this book that social isn't a destination, it is a journey. Social is a changing space, with people bringing out new platforms, the move to messaging, but the reluctance of people to leave e-mail behind. The markets you work in all have an impact on the relative impact and usage in your organization.

This highest stage of social selling maturity is where actions are measured, not to police the employees but to see what is working and what is not. Organizations will work in a closed loop, continually experimenting and innovating with employees and customers alike.

Good questions you could ask yourself are:

- Where have we had success using networks and community?
- What relationships should we be using in the future?
- Which content is the most effective? Do we need to make changes?
- Do we use the terminology of the community and influencers or do we create our own?
- What target companies or individuals are underrepresented or over-saturated?
- How can we work in our networks during the deal cycle to get the best coverage, wider and deeper?

- How can we affect influencers (external and within an account) to help us grow our share of wallet?

- Do we have the social graph of our accounts mapped out, showing internal and external influence? Do we have these bases covered?

Social initiatives

There are various social initiatives that will be kicked off at different stages of this maturity model and we will now look at each one of these to explain how they fit in, where they work and where they don't work. We look at:

- the importance of sales and marketing working together;

- providing content that can be used in an employee advocacy programme;

- clear delivery of messaging out into the channel so that channel partners, alliance partners and value-added resellers can use the same messaging;

- how marketing automation should help salespeople spend more time in front of clients.

Sales and marketing – Smarketing

In many corporations sales and marketing just don't get along. Sales say that the leads that marketing create are no good, and marketing say that sales don't follow up the leads that are generated.

This is often because the two sides are too busy throwing stones at each other to sit down and understand each other's wants and needs. Defining a lead is a great place to start. How many meetings have you sat in where people have talked about leads, but they are really just business cards from a conference?

On the other hand, a lead isn't a company that is just about to sign for your product and service. Sometimes sales seem to think that unless a prospect is about to put pen to paper and effort is required, it's a waste of time.

We have seen the use of social to collaborate as a great way of bringing the two sides together. Think of it as a corporate Facebook, where an event can be a Facebook group. Only the people involved in the event are part of the group and all sides can collaborate. It also reduces the amount of e-mail traffic that gets pumped out to lists and never read, leading to better and timely cooperation on events.

Employee advocate programme

This was partly alluded to above, and there are now suppliers that offer platforms that can be rolled out for employees. Often these are seen by employers as ways of pumping out content, with no thought to the quality of the content or the consequences.

The supplier's argument is simple; people will believe an employee more than a brand. Yes sure, but we are back to the 'he/she would say that, they work there' argument. Unless people are trained on what good content looks like and a structured programme is in place then it is unlikely to move the needle.

In our experience these programmes are often rolled out when companies are in the 'random acts of social' phase. The employees tend to have a follower count on Twitter and a LinkedIn profile consisting mainly of work colleagues or ex-work colleagues, now with competitors. You have this zero-sum game where content (and we have no idea if it's any good as we are not measuring it) is pumped out to other colleagues or into the hands of the competition. We think this is a waste of time.

It is not until we get into the 'structured programme' phase that people understand they need to grow their networks, and it is then that such programmes can be used to prospect and nurture.

Channel partner advocacy

If you have a channel or value-added reseller (VAR) programme these people are often too small to create their own content and would relish getting posts from the 'mother ship'. That is, the content can have a parent and child relationship. The parent supplies official content and the children can decide to put this out through their channels. There are tools you can use to automate this.

This means the parent can get content out through its employees, and the channel and their employees, increasing significantly reach and amplification.

Now the 'let's throw mud at the wall and hope it sticks' people will be rubbing their hands in glee. We have seen such programmes where I was shown a report and was told, 'Look how many partners we have signed up'. I agreed they had done a good job. Then I pointed out a column in the report, which was the number of retweets, and the figure was zero for every partner. As with the employee advocate programme, unless there is a clear training programme for all partners explaining why they are doing this, you are literally flushing money down the toilet.

Influencer marketing

Over the last year this has become all the rage and there are different platforms that can offer a list of your influencers.

Let's go back to basics here; today there are online and offline influencers. Journalists, for example, are influencers who will have an online presence but their main channel to market is through their newspaper or periodical. They are therefore still pretty much an offline influencer. So don't forget, the online tools look great but you still need to cover all your bases.

The other 'gotcha' we see is that influencers are seen as sales targets, or an influence event is seen as a sales event. These are often run in an analogue format.

First and foremost an influencer programme has no end. It is a continued process of nurture and most likely a long game.

So what is influencer marketing?

A primary objective of an effective marketing department is marketplace visibility. The team needs to build awareness for a product, company, or other positive change.

But often awareness isn't enough. How can marketing move beyond mere visibility to engage customers, generate leads, or encourage purchase behaviour? One tactic for generating influence is to 'borrow' it from those experts or individuals who already have the ability to persuade or move customers to take action.

Successful influencer marketing isn't just about paying boldfaced names or social media stars. It has its own nuances. People love to have a third-party view on any discussion, especially if that person is independent. In the past people turned to companies such as Gartner or Forrester but in the 'new world' of social, a new independent person has emerged that has a viewpoint. The blogger.

Bloggers are generally not connected to any major product or brand and are therefore seen as trusted advisors.

Influencer marketing is about getting influencers to say 'nice' things about your brand. When buyers are in the buying process the influencer might say, 'You must have product XYZ on your shortlist'.

We all make decisions based on trust or how much we trust somebody as part of our buyer process. From a marketing perspective, trust and control are at different ends of the scale. We place a certain amount of trust in a salesperson or an employee advocate, but we would probably think there might be a level of bias. That said, marketing may be highly controlling the message, which gives a lower level of trust for the buyer and a high level of control for the marketer.

As we move up the spectrum of customer advocacy the level of control for the marketer goes down, but as buyers we are more likely to trust customer comments.

The next level of marketing you should introduce is to get your channel partner to market for you. Again, the charge of 'they would say that' can be levelled against you, but often these partners may be trusted advisors at a customer or account level.

Customer advocates are a key component to the marketing mix. While you can expect people to support their decisions, sometimes the people who have advocated for you can turn and speak against you. But if managed properly these individuals can be harnessed to provide input into product development and innovation as well as saying nice things about you.

We know a person who is a MicroScooter product advocate and he is proud of the product and the changes he has enabled. He tells me about it all the time and now I am telling you. That is great marketing.

Influencer marketing offers the highest level of trust for the buyer but the lowest level of control for marketing.

In previous chapters we talked about going to a networking event and we asked whether we would stand in front of everybody and say, 'Buy my product!' No we wouldn't. But we've seen influencer programmes run in a similar way.

'How will you run your influencer programme?' I asked the global head of social selling. She told me she would use a tool to find the influencer and then give the salesperson a piece of content and ask them to make contact. It's worth mentioning that this company was in the 'random acts of social' stage. I'm amazed that an influencer didn't tweet, 'Some idiot from company XYZ has just tried to pass me off with some boring white paper'.

We have also seen influencer events that were actually sales events, run very much like events in the analogue world. A senior VP would be running the event, but they had no social profile. I'm sure the event generated leads but did it generate influence?

I'm aware of 'independent' social media celebrities who are paid to say good things about certain brands. Influencer marketing is very real, but it is not for this book to go into its pros and cons.

Marketing automation

There are whole books on marketing automation so we are not going to cover this subject in depth, but we do recommend that an organization embraces marketing automation to support the social selling process.

Marketing automation is actually a misnomer. A marketer once said to me, 'The marketing automation tool is nothing to do with marketing, it's a sales tool'. When I asked the head of sales who was responsible for the marketing automation tool, he looked at me quizzically and said, 'It's in the name, marketing are'.

That's where you can see that sales and marketing working together is so key.

So as a salesperson how can marketing automation help you and free you up to have more customer meetings?

As a salesperson, one of my weekly jobs is what I call 'plate spinning'. You must have seen one of those circus acts where a person has sticks and on top of the sticks are plates. The trick is that the performer keeps spinning the plates so that none fall off.

We have all come across the person that says, 'I love what you are saying but it's year end, month end etc, call me back in three, six months'. Marketing automation is where you get people to opt in and the system takes them through a nurture process, the theory being that in three or six months a lead pops out. On the basis that I probably spend half a day a week 'plate spinning', marketing automation has freed me up to get additional customer meetings and saves me that half a day.

Note: the trick is building the marketing automation process to really nurture the prospect and not just to be a catapult to throw white papers at them. As we say, this can be covered in another book.

Marketing automation is often seen as a marketing project as part of a modern marketing programme, which means it is often introduced in a silo within marketing, without taking sales along with them. But if it is introduced as part of a company-wide digital programme it can be integrated with all the other social programmes taking place.

Summary

In this chapter we have shared with you the maturity stages companies go through as they transform into digital organizations and implement social selling.

Organizations have to realize that the move to digital and social is a change in behaviour. Such changes require a programme, help from changemakers and a plan to embed the programme into day-to-day working.

This won't happen overnight and a company shouldn't expect that employees will become social sellers just by saying they are. Change can take time and organizations should use the model to recognize where they are, and help accelerate their maturity by driving a strategy, rather than a series of tactics such as 'random acts of social'.

Five steps to getting you started

10

This book so far has provided you with the theory as well as some practice to help you move from the world of analogue to digital selling. Before we talk about social selling and the future here is a methodology to follow with the end point of you becoming a social seller.

The Changemaker Method

The 'Changemaker Method' is our methodology that describes how social sales teams operate differently to traditional sales teams; this can be visualized as five steps along a path (as shown in Figure 10.1):

- **Step 1:** Setting up shop – how to prepare the salespeople so that they can be discovered.
- **Step 2:** Learning to listen – how to listen to what is happening in the wider network to scale up that discoverability.
- **Step 3:** Building authority and influence – how to build up authority and influence so that the changemaker will select the salesperson to be part of their team.
- **Step 4:** Optimizing – how to use technology to optimize the sales process.

- **Step 5:** Enhancing collaboration – how to bring connected economy ideas into the organization so that it becomes more agile and flexible.

When taken together, the five steps define the path that needs to be taken to achieve the required organizational change to make social selling work. This is another very important point to understand early on. Shifting to a social selling model successfully relies on organizational change, specifically organizational change which is in tune with the shift in buyer behaviour as discussed at the start of this book.

FIGURE 10.1 Changemaker Method Steps

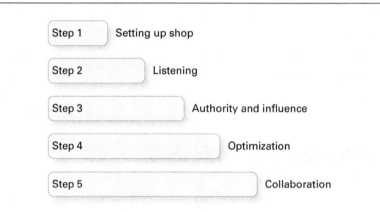

A common mistake sales teams make is to regard social selling as something that can be 'spread' on top of how they currently work. Because we're talking about a sociological shift caused by the tipping point of mass adoption of the internet that has caused a change in buyer behaviour, the organization has to change its behaviour and culture. Staying the same isn't an option here, because if you stay the same you're essentially saying, 'The internet doesn't have an effect on how people work together', which self-evidently isn't true.

That's not to say you cannot pilot these ideas on a smaller scale – you absolutely must – but your final implementation must be couched as organizational change.

Getting started

We'll assume that at this point you are looking to run a pilot, and that you need to test and explore the ideas in this book. There are some initial pieces you will need to put into place. One change you will need to make straight away is to bring the marketing and sales teams closer together. Traditionally these teams tend to sit at opposite sides of the office and throw rocks at each other. You need to change that; see the online bonus material for Chapter 7, 'Why sales and marketing departments need to work together for a common purpose'.

Social selling works by exposing individuals within the business on social networks. A common mistake people make is to assume that companies have any importance at all in social selling. They generally don't. Your changemaker wants to involve a person in their team, not a business. The fact they work for company XYZ is in some ways harmful because the changemaker is looking to manage out bias, and so the salesperson may be less attractive just because they work for such-and-such a company. The changemaker is very much in 'salesperson avoidance mode'.

(This changes at the point of implementation because the business then moves into a mode where capability overrides bias. The business will want to engage a supply partner with a proven brand, proven track record, etc in order to manage out risk.)

Social salespeople therefore need to be adept at marketing because they are selling themselves and their own authority and credibility into the changemaker's social network, with some support from their employer's reputation and branding. A social salesperson must soften the market in the same way a marketing team would, preparing the ground with skilfully positioned messages that aid discoverability.

A changemaker won't listen to 'Hi, I'm Bob from XYZ plc' because the changemaker doesn't 'see' the 'XYZ plc' part. A changemaker wants to hear 'Hi, I'm Bob, and hey did you see this reputation I personally have in the area of hosted telephony?'

Most salespeople will need help in improving this skill, and that help is more easily obtained if marketing and sales have a closer, more collegiate relationship. Some people create neologisms to describe this new aggregated team, such as 'Smarketing', or 'Smales': the merger of sales and marketing.

Secondly, even in very large organizations, you will only find one person who really gets this whole idea and can act as a champion (this might be you). You're looking for someone who is a 'white tiger', in other words, very rare. They need to understand the sociological changes that have created a change in buyer behaviour, they have to be able to work within the connected economy as if they were born into it, but they absolutely must have respect from the organization as being someone who is a changemaker and has over-delivered to the business time and time again.

You need that person who will run with it, make the whole idea work, and have the trust of the organization so that when it comes time to make this larger scale permanent change, senior management will believe it will work.

A word of warning – in 10 years' time that person will almost certainly be the sales director of your business.

Step 1: Setting up shop

Salespeople have always known that the sales process centres around people. When we say, 'Go out there and find opportunities', we're not proposing hunting around in the dirt in the way a pig might hunt for truffles. Opportunities are always 'attached' to people, and generally speaking the more people the salesperson deals with the more opportunities they will find.

Given that opportunities are attached to people, and given that changemakers don't see corporate allegiances, setting up shop is much more like setting up multiple franchises as opposed to one huge, flagship, cornerstone-of-the-mall type of shop.

You will need exactly one franchise – exactly one shop – per salesperson, and the first practical step on the path (Changemaker Method Step 1) is to set up these shops.

Each shop needs to be branded as belonging to the individual salesperson, and this needs to be done in a way that aids discovery to the changemaker who is looking for a particular mix of skills and capability. 'Bob, the expert in hosted telephony, who happens to work for company XYZ (the leading supplier of hosted telephony services)', is the correct cadence here. It's 'Bob' – it's personal. He's 'an expert' – he's attractive to the changemaker who's trying to build an ad hoc team to ideate a solution. Finally, 'he works for company XYZ' – however, this part comes into play more when it comes to the 'beauty parade' part of the sales process when the supplier is chosen.

Social selling is 'bigger' than the social networks that we use today. At the moment, we have some services that we can use, but we have to assume that in the long term the presence and/or usefulness of those tools will change. Today, the tool you need to use in the first instance is LinkedIn. Remember, social selling is the result of sociological change, so in terms of strategy you need to be thinking in generational timescales. IT services pop into and out of existence very quickly over those timescales.

But back to LinkedIn for now. The most important thing to sort in the first instance with regards to LinkedIn is to get a picture up, and a summary. This is where marketing can help, because that summary has to be customer-centric and social selling friendly.

A mistake here would be to just have marketing come up with one summary that is copied and pasted to each salesperson. Each one needs to be authentic and natural and in the salesperson's own voice. But it needs to be done in a way that encourages discoverability and connection, and is in line with the organization's marketing strategy. This is why marketing needs to be closely involved.

The way to do this is to keep drilling down from 'corporate' to 'personal'. Get the marketing team to work with each person as if each one were a separate client with distinct needs.

The next stage is something that traditional salespeople find very hard – they have to engage with the network. This means they need to be posting content they find online (content curation), creating original content (content creation), prospecting for new people to talk to, and engaging with other people on the network (amplification – sharing, liking; or direct conversations). If they don't do this, to keep stretching the metaphor, the doors are locked and the shutters are down. The 'shop' is only 'open' if the salesperson is engaging.

Traditional salespeople will struggle with this. Most salespeople know if they make a certain number of calls, they'll get a certain number of meetings, then a certain number of opportunities, then a certain number of deals. For them, the phone calls are what keep the shop open. Telling them to stop making the calls and start spending that same time on LinkedIn – that's a huge ask for a salesperson. You'll have to manage that.

We suggest that as a rule of thumb, salespeople spend around six hours a week on this type of direct activity on the social networks in the beginning. That is going to seem like a lot. However, it's essential this happens.

Depending on the salesperson, they may also wish to take this approach over to Twitter. B2B social selling works extremely well on Twitter as this network evolved from the ground up to actually support the process of ideation, but it's very much a 'second stage'.

Step 2: Learning to listen

At this point we have a group of salespeople all with their own 'shop', who keep that shop open by posting links to other people's content, posting their original content, and working to develop connection via conversations.

The next step (Changemaker Method Step 2) is to start scaling the process out. In particular, you now need to solve the classic social selling problem of the salesperson asking, 'How do I talk to someone I don't know?'

The approach that kills social selling stone dead is, ironically, to do any proactive selling. Remember our changemaker – they're trying to build a team, and you want to be part of it, but the changemaker a) doesn't know what they want yet as they're still ideating a solution, and b) doesn't want to hear 'biased' messages from suppliers at this point. If the changemaker says, 'Hey guys, can you help me understand why phone calls keep being dropped?', the social salesperson must not at this stage say, '10 Per Cent Off Hosted Telephony Solutions – Offer Must End Monday!'

Whilst the salesperson is working LinkedIn as per the above, they will naturally be having conversations. For example, if they share a post someone else has written on the benefits of hosted telephony, the original author may say, 'Hey, thanks for sharing my post'. The salesperson can then say, 'No problem – I thought it was interesting, especially the part about ABC, but I wasn't sure about the XYZ part?' From that point, a conversation can flow, and a relationship can be developed.

The challenge there is that for a traditional salesperson, that connection is 'wasteful' in terms of their time. The person who wrote the article is unlikely to drop an opportunity into the sales funnel, so why bother talking to them? However, social selling operates much more like networking and the trick is to build up a good deal of high-quality connections regardless of whether those people are likely to become your direct customers. We'll talk much more about trust, authority, and influence in a later section, but for now any relationship with someone who has authority and influence within their chosen space is valuable to a social salesperson, regardless of whether they have a burning desire to drop an opportunity into the sales funnel.

The second step is to start adding scale, and this means listening to what's happening on the social network and responding, as opposed to broadcasting a message to the market and listening and reacting to the response.

This is an area that traditional salespeople typically do not understand. They are used to working through lists trying interruptions typically crafted along the same proven message until someone bites. This is the classic sales mantra of 'if you ask enough boys/girls at a dance to dance, someone will dance'.

A traditional salesperson would approach all 50 people with the same broadcast message – 'Come Dance With Me! Offer Must End Midnight!'

This is where marketing comes in to the sales process again, because what's needed is a 'microcrafting' of position messages on a one-to-one basis. Of the 50 people you could ask to dance, find the one that looks a little nervous and go to them with a 'confidence' message: 'Come on, I'm really good at dancing, we'll have a good time!' To the second person who exudes confidence: 'I'm really good at dancing. Are you as good at dancing as I think you are?' The result is the same (you get to dance), the position is the same ('I'm good at dancing!'), but the message is different. In the digital world, personalization of message is key.

To an extent, this method is a result of the traditional salesperson having only a small amount of information available to them before they deliver the message. All they may have is a name, a company name, and a phone number. But with social media, prospects are telegraphing information all the time, and this information coming from the prospect allows the social salesperson to microcraft and retarget their positioning message.

Plus, it stops them having to ask 50 people on the off chance that two say yes. They can concentrate on the two they know they can craft a good message for and just approach them.

I'll restate that as it's a particularly important point. Social selling is about carefully approaching the right people, slowly and in a considered fashion, one to one, with the correct message. It is not about plastering a 'good enough' message over a huge audience, hoping one will be interrupted in such a way that they bite. The total elapsed effort, in terms of time, should net out to be the same for both traditional and social selling methods.

As we talk about in the book, when you walk into a room of 100 people, using social networks you should have already worked out the 20 people useful to you.

One of the challenges to salespeople who are new to social media in general is that this can feel a little creepy. Those people tend to think of this as 'stalking'. It really isn't. People posting on social networks – even when that post is personal – want the audience; they want the attention in exactly the same way a playwright wants people to go and see their plays. A playwright doesn't write a play in the hope no one will go and see the opening night! They write it in the hope every man, woman, and dog in the country will go and see it.

Listening also applies to competitors. One of the dark secrets about social selling is that because your salespeople are operating out in public, everyone can see what they are doing including your competitors. It's perfectly easy, especially on Twitter, to monitor conversations and map connections. As soon as you identify top social salespeople at your competitors, you can see who they are talking to and listen to the conversations. The information gleaned from that activity can only ever be useful.

Then, if you're particularly Machiavellian, do feel free to find the top social salespeople at your competitors' and poach them!

Step 3: Building authority and influence

At this point we have a collection of salespeople who have set up their own individual shops, they're active on their social networks and keeping the shop running, and they're learning how to turn their attention out from their immediate environment through social listening. At this point, they're starting to scale.

The next thing that we need to do is to start building up influence and authority (Changemaker Method Step 3).

Although this is midway through our five-step plan to change the organization, it is the final step in the maturation task the individual salesperson has to complete in order to become a social salesperson. Once they do this, the individual has completed their changes and can turn to optimizing their own social selling skills. The final two steps in the Changemaker Method look to change and optimize the organization.

Recall that the changemaker ultimately is trying to build an ad hoc team that is given the task of ideating a solution to a business problem. The changemaker chooses members of the team based on trust. The salesperson's job is to exude enough trust through the social network that the changemaker chooses them to be part of the team. The first two steps – setting up shop and listening – go towards making the salesperson discoverable. This third step is about making them trustable. The changemaker says, 'You seem to know what you're doing – can you help us with this problem about dropping calls?' The 'You' can only happen if they have been discovered; the 'seem to know what you're doing' comes from trust, and that comes from influence and authority.

Building authority and influence is actually very easy. You need to be putting messages out into the network that deliver value. This is done through content curation and content creation.

Content curation is where you find information that might be of use to people who you want to have relationships with and put it out into your social network. The idea is that if you say to your contacts, 'Hey everyone, here's a great piece on the risks around hosted telephony implementation', you're offering something up on the understanding that it might be helpful. Social networks exist within the connected economy, and the currency of the connected economy is appreciation. If you deliver value to someone by pointing them at some interesting content, that person will 'pay' for that value by increasing your authority.

Think about it, if somebody retweets your content, you are going to feel inwardly pleased with that and that person. If they make a comment about how good your content is and amplify that through your network then (hopefully) you will make a mental note that the person is 'good'.

The mechanism by which this happens is they (at a baseline level) amplify your message by sharing or retweeting, or they will 'pay more' by actually going out into their network and advocating you. 'Hey everyone, Bob/Brenda shared this great piece on XYZ – you should follow them.'

Content curation is by far the easiest thing to do when it comes to building authority and influence, and this should be happening on a daily basis. The nature of these networks is that posting a lot of curated content is perfectly OK – if it's on message. If you have 1,000 people in your network, and you curate 10 links a day, they are not getting 'spammed' each with 10 links a day. It'll appear on their timeline and if they happen to look at their timeline when you post something they'll see it. Timelines and news streams on social networks are something that people dip in and out of, so don't fear posting a lot. (You should, however, fear posting the same physical message again and again. Don't do that because that will come across as spam and it'll cause people to opt out from your network.)

However, content curation only gets you so far. Effectiveness of content curation can be measured by how much you are being amplified, and from there you can use amplification to gauge authority and influence. Those measures tell you that you are delivering value, which is obviously good.

But if you want to deliver more value, you have to be delivering unique ideas into the network, and this means you need to be creating content. You can create whatever content you like – blogging is very easy. Video blogging is also easy, and is sufficiently 'new and shiny' enough that in relation to blogging the same ideas should get amplified more through video channels. (We believe the future of content is video, so if you have an appetite to get into this early, you should.) But it might be that you can create content on Pinterest, or Snapchat, or Instagram. The channel or packaging is not important – what's important is that ideas are novel, original and create curiosity in the reader to find out more about you.

(Also, don't be worried about using the 'wrong' sort of channel for B2B. If you run a network cabling business and want to put (with permission) photos of particularly good cabling jobs on Instagram, go right ahead. The changemaker doesn't care where this stuff is. All you want is for the changemaker to look at it and go, 'That's a neat cabling job – I should get to know that person!')

It is likely that in a team of salespeople, not everyone will want to do this, or indeed be able to do it. Creating content is a skill in itself, and creating good content is difficult. As a manager, we'd recommend finding the one or two people who can actually make a decent job of it and a) encourage them and b) give them the freedom to do it. We are aware of a sales guy whose dog has 2,000 followers on Twitter. Embrace this.

This will seem like a lot of work, but the reality is that this aspect is essential to reaching a broad audience. You ultimately want each salesperson and the greater sales team as 'attractors' to the changemakers out there in your chosen space. They are looking for initial value by way of information as an indicator of trustability. If you provide that, and you have salespeople who are able to have meaningful conversations with those people they meet on social networks, you're home and dry.

Step 4: Optimizing

At this point, the individual salesperson's job is complete and, as mentioned, they will be in a place of optimizing what they do. They have a shop, they have a network that they are developing relationships in, they are scaling out that network by using listening, and they are building authority and influence through content curation and possibly through content creation. At this point, they are social selling.

The next steps look at improving the organization's capability at executing social selling. This step (Changemaker Step 4) is about starting to fill in support to the sales team and giving them tools to optimize around this new way of working.

Generally in social sales the process of nurturing a lead to close doesn't change from how it worked in traditional sales. You still need to qualify the lead into an opportunity. You still need to have meetings and conversations, develop the solution into an implementation plan, and then look attractive enough so that the customer chooses you to deliver the final product.

In all complex sales, the sales cycle is long, and there will be points within that cycle where you're not actively selling but instead you're keeping the prospect warm. You can remove some of that burden from the sales team by implementing some automation. Think of automation as a little robot who can do some of the 'keep warm' activities whilst the prospect is making their way around the sales cycle. It's the easiest way to start optimizing your social selling process.

Automation allows you to send out messages automatically to customers over and above the messages they'll be receiving from individual salespeople as part of the day-to-day activity on social networks. (Remember the prospect will be in the salesperson's network so there is some natural incubation going on in that regard anyway.) What you're looking to do here is gently underscore the trust and authority that's been built whilst the prospect does the arduous and long job of getting their organization into a position where they can buy what you sell.

This is the part where you'll need to investigate tools and design those tools' implementation in line with the marketing and sales strategy. We make our suggestions in Chapter 8. To make everything holistic, you may well find the best way to bring those tools in is to be a changemaker yourself and engage your own social network, as one of your target changemakers would.

A particular point of caution here is that if you do this badly, the 'voice' that comes through will be inauthentic. An inauthentic voice – an overly robotic, obviously automated voice – is an anathema on social media. An inauthentic voice indicates that messages are not being individually 'microcrafted' as we discussed before, and it will cause a decrease in authority, and a knock-on decrease in influence.

In short, it's possible to do automation very badly, but it's equally possible to do it very well and use technology to optimize the social sales process.

Step 5: Enhancing collaboration

At this point individual salespeople are acting as social salespeople, and the sales organization is starting to discover and deploy tools and procedures to support this new way of working.

The final step on the path (Changemaker Method Step 5) represents scaling out of the collaboration that you have created between the sales and marketing teams and starting to take it out to other departments and channel partner organizations. It represents the transformation of the entire business to one that 'plays nicely' with the connected economy.

Organizations traditionally have been set up in a way that pre-dates the connected economy – ie they are mostly hierarchical (top-down management), and mostly siloed off into separate departments. Those departments tend to be operated in a reasonably procedural fashion. All of this makes sense – businesses are like sausage machines; all you have to do is crank the handle, the machinery turns and raw meat goes in one side and sausages come out the other. That process of transformation is how value gets delivered, and profit is given as reward for that value.

The idea of the connected economy is to allow people to work together in a more natural and fluid way. At the end of the day, we're all people who are looking to work together and do a good job. Take two businesses that want to work together as customer and supplier. In reality, it's not and never has been the two businesses that want to work together; it's human beings who happen to be employed by one side or the other that want to work together.

This is the first principle of the connected economy – stripping away organizational boundaries and allowing people to do the job they need to do in the best way they can. Those boundaries can be internal (as we have said before about needing to bring sales and marketing together), or they can be external (as in the example above, of two business).

Businesses that are very rigid, partitioned and siloed, with lots of boundaries, are very inflexible. Connected economy ideas 'plasticize' inflexible businesses, making them more able to react and adapt. In our opinion, all businesses should operate internally, with suppliers, partners, and customers, as connected economy entities, which is why we say that enhancing this capability to collaborate completes the organization's journey from traditional selling to social selling.

Summary

In this chapter we took you through a thorough grounding in the 'how' of social selling. We started by looking at the five steps of the Changemaker Method – setting up shop, learning to listen, building authority and influence, optimizing the process and enhancing collaboration. Importantly we discussed how social selling had to be introduced as a complete organizational change, as opposed to something just to be 'spread' on top of the sales process. We then drilled into a detail of each one, looking at practical ideas that you can use to start delivering results from social selling.

This methodology enables teams to get social selling, to break through the mantra of personal branding and really start building their own communities and influence.

Yes, this requires us to change the way we work, but it is our belief that we need to disrupt ourselves in the connected economy.

Conclusion

In this book we hope you have seen that analogue selling has changed, along with social selling and personal branding. In this book we hope you see the emergence of Social Selling 2.0.

Digital selling is no longer about a LinkedIn profile giving you the competitive edge. An amazing LinkedIn profile won't pay the rent. A sale, after all, is about leads, sales pursuits and winning deals to create revenue and profit.

As the digital landscape has changed buyer habits, it is increasingly difficult to reach them early enough in their decision-making process using traditional sales methods. Developing relationships with decision makers through social networks has become an increasingly critical skill – enabling sales professionals to engage early on and 'hack' the buying process.

Social Selling provides a practical, step-by-step blueprint for harnessing these specifics and we hope you have enjoyed these proven techniques, including:

- how to use networks purposefully to build social trust and create a high-quality community;

- how to develop real influence and authority in your subject area and connect with changemakers;

- how to scale the social selling strategy across an organization, including maturity and investment models, risk and governance, and technology platforms.

In addition we have outlined what we think is essential reading for sales professionals, digital sales directors and SMEs (subject matter experts) who want to embrace the power of social selling in their organization. Regardless of whether your company is big or small, or B2B or B2C, you now should have:

- a 'how to', providing a clear, step-by-step blueprint for social selling success based on building authority and influence in target communities;

- practical and proven advice borne of hard-won experience rolling out these techniques across large sales forces;

- an outline of how to roll this strategy out across an organization, including investment, risk and governance, and working across teams and technology platforms.

The day we sat in a coffee shop in London and came up with the idea for this book is still etched in our memories. We both felt that the arguments for social selling hadn't moved forward in four years and at the time of writing they still haven't.

The subject matter was all about the start of the sales process and demand generation; there was nobody writing about how to use social and digital during the sales pursuit.

In fact, the whole subject had been (and we don't mean to offend any marketers reading) hijacked by the marketing department, because people see them as demand generators and therefore surely social selling all sits with them?

Our other observation of social selling was that it was all about creating a personal brand, which we felt was all very 'so what?' Or people were talking about social selling as being about a tool such as LinkedIn.

When we pitched the idea to our publisher Kogan Page, they went away and did a review of social selling books. We breathed a sigh of relief when they came back and said, 'We don't want a book on personal branding; there are already too many books on this subject'. The fact that we were going to completely change the narrative about the use of social and digital selling was what got us the book deal.

If there is one thing we can predict with certainty it is that there will always be change taking place in the world of social and digital. Social or digital selling is very much in its infancy, and people will think up more and more ways to use tools to help find influencers, change agents and buyers within accounts.

That said, there are some things that won't change. We have always said that selling has not changed with the introduction of digital. Yes, maybe there are new methods, but we are still looking for people in our accounts and then trying to build rapport with them. It is now just easier to do this using online techniques.

We also don't foresee a complete switch to social; it will run parallel to and complement the use of the phone and e-mail. I'm sorry, but people who tell you that cold calling is dead are wrong, and are in fact being detrimental to the sales profession, as people believe them. If you find a way to create business using 100 per cent social, please contact us and let us know.

By reading this book, you are gaining significant competitive advantage through being able to implement this strategy ahead of the competition. I'm sure your competitors will be sitting in a meeting one day with their sales figures gradually going downwards and ask, 'Where did that come from?'

With the evolvement in social and digital, so too do you need to evolve the ideas we have written about in this book. If everybody is creating an online community, then what moves the needle anymore?

We therefore see an 'arms race' in online techniques, and in fact companies will start seeing the strategies, behaviours and techniques they employ as being what makes them up. Online will become part of a company's DNA. We are not aware (yet) of any company that has built social and digital into the terms and conditions of an employment contract. People have rules about contacting customers and using physical assets, but not digital assets.

For example, say you work for company A and they pay for your LinkedIn profile, and during your time working for them in sales you build a strong community and network. If you leave company A and go to their competitor, who now owns that asset?

In the United States people already have separate personal and work LinkedIn and Twitter accounts. Or will this just become seen as 'noise' that we move from role to role and company to company? In the old days, people took their Rolodex or 'black book' of contacts with them, and companies didn't do anything then.

The future of personal branding

Personal branding is great but it has key limitations. Yes, people will look you up before a meeting and make a judgment on what you are like and how that meeting will go; interesting, boring... They will do that by looking at the blogs you have written, the industry knowledge you can demonstrate, and most of all, whether it looks like you can help them.

While a few 'corporate articles' will be OK, being the echo chamber of your company PR department is going to look pretty boring. In fact, because it will look like you obviously cannot have your own opinions or an open view, I doubt the person in that meeting will trust what you say. The expectation is that you will just be talking the company line. But people want help, they need to be educated.

Over the next few years, people will realize that we cannot all be a thought leader, and therefore to expect everybody to strive to be so is a waste of everybody's time. That said, there does seem to be a rise of the 'corporate nominee thought leader'. As corporations move up the social maturity model, they suddenly realize they have 'social champions' and 'change agents'. But what they won't have done is nurture this talent. So they do one of three things, using what are known as black hat techniques (the baddies in cowboy movies always wore black hats, and the good guys wore white).

The first would be for a corporation to socially promote a vice president (VP) or senior person, but with somebody else running their social for them. My advice to anybody reading this is, if you suspect any person of having their social run for them, ask them questions. Ask them online and when you see them about the material they have posted. You can soon see the charlatans.

The second thing corporations do is promoting people who have little or no social footprint; usually they are cajoled into writing corporate articles under the pretence they are writing for themselves. This often works for a short while and is done as part of a project to increase 'share of voice'. Let's not forget that 'share of voice' is a measure of how much mud you can throw at a wall, the aim being to throw more than the competition. This is great, but we're not sure how many leads it creates.

Sometimes good does come out of this, though, as often just forcing people to blog means they gain confidence and then find their voice.

The Rolling Stones started as a covers band until their manager locked Mick Jagger and Keith Richards in a room and told them he wouldn't let them out until they had written a song.

The third thing that companies do is bring in outside talent, in the belief that they don't have social talent within the company.

Companies have to get better at finding and nurturing talent internally. This is something you cannot force. People are believable thought leaders or they are not. People either want to be and have a passion to be a thought leader or they don't. Somebody once asked us in a meeting, 'So how do I find these people in my company?' The answer is very simple; you will find them online.

For us, personal branding has a 'high watermark' (apart from being likeable online) that people need to be looking to achieve: gaining inbound traffic.

What do we mean by that? This is where people are approaching you, the ultimate being a request about your products and services. But then again it could be a speaker request.

One sales guy we trained was almost a blank canvas, as the company he had previously worked for didn't do social. We helped him rewrite his LinkedIn profile from scratch, and explained how to use LinkedIn to build a community and nurture a platform. He rang me up one day when a prospect of his liked a graphic he had posted. It was a great example of cause and effect, and this was the start for him of a journey in social, personal branding and the aim of inbound and influence.

Talking with strangers

In Chapter 3 on talking to strangers we discussed how social, in a way, goes against everything our parents told us, which was never to talk to strangers. Social and networking requires us to work in teams and collaborate, but it also requires us to talk to people we don't know.

As we discussed, networking for networking's sake has a very low return, as we can end up talking to people who are of little or no use to us.

We have to get better at finding the right people and having the right conversations with people. There are no excuses not to have found out about somebody before you meet him or her.

The clever bit is still about finding and focusing on who the right people are to talk to. Influence has many guises. In the previous chapters we have talked about how influence on your territory can come from outside your territory. A person might have left one of your accounts, but prospects may still call up for his or her advice and guidance.

There is a view that the territories of the future will be allocated based on who you know and the community you have built rather than the usual postal/zip codes, etc.

Having a visualization of a salesperson's influence and network would be a great tool to have. Let's not forget, if you told a salesperson you were measuring them on their LinkedIn contacts, they would link to everybody on LinkedIn just to make a land grab.

If you could measure a salesperson's network, influence and community based on amplification, engagement and interaction then that would be useful. Better still would be if you could do this across multiple social graphs and see it visualized. This would certainly help (along with a sales track record and excellent references) recruit the 'A-players' of the future. I'm sure companies would pay for this as there would be a great business case for reducing the number of failed recruits and enabling salespeople to get selling quicker.

I'm aware of people who do use Klout as a measure of social, but at the time of writing this measure does not really seem to have progressed in recent years. There are network visualization tools, but these seem to be based on the number of connections (easily scammed) and not real influence.

Growing your network

People often ask us, how do we measure progress? Currently, unless you use SSI and Klout there is little in the way of measurement to say yes, you have moved from having no influence to having a bit of influence. You can, of course, get a 'finger in the air', maybe by your number of followers, if a customer has liked your blog, or you have an SSI of 72.

The difficulty is that influence crosses many social networks and extends, whether you like it or not, into Facebook, Instagram, e-mail, etc. Wouldn't it be great, as a recruiting company (and also as a salesperson) to have a way to measure a salesperson's influence, network and community?

At the time of writing I understand that LinkedIn is looking to map connections and networks (we use the term network and not community) in LinkedIn. This is more about helping sales teams or companies where they have multiple salespeople selling into the one account.

When we played football (soccer) at school, the whole group of us ran round the ball hoping to get a kick. Then somebody introduced us to passing and marking and suddenly the game changed. This is the objective we have always wanted to achieve through team selling, and maybe through LinkedIn we will.

But that still does not allow us to see the influence on our accounts from externals.

Changemakers

Changemakers are people in accounts who have influence but probably have little authority.

In our experience, organizations are becoming more reliant on them for decisions. Many boards of directors have realized that they don't 'get' social and that they need people they can rely on to help them make the move to a digital business. As we covered in the chapter on risk, just getting your intern to do the social may be low cost but could have a negative impact on your brand.

Changemakers, therefore, are seen as being social but also having the business acumen to know what makes a good social media post and which post will see the world come crashing down around your ears.

As they further enhance this role, and become mentors to sales, marketing and management, we see them becoming the leaders of the future.

As suppliers, you need to be seeking out changemakers and nurturing their talent so they can lead the social projects that will implement the strategies in this book, which will create leads, revenue and competitive advantage.

In sales pursuits, you need to be looking out for them and bringing them onside to your campaign. In fact, we think that without access to a changemaker you won't make a sale.

LinkedIn figures say that on average 5.4 people in any organization are needed within the company to make a sale. Companies such as this have a requirement for multiple people to make a decision. Internally for a company this works as it lessens (by spreading) the risk of a wrong decision being made. Most people understand that nowadays you need consensus in any decision.

But any decision for your product or service will most likely require a level of change, be it a change in supplier or a change in the way people will work. Naturally people don't like change, and you may well therefore come across people who will block or stop your proposal. They may even tell you they like your proposal but still try to block it.

That is why we see changemakers as people who can see a tangible benefit to your product and service. You still need to follow the same routes, build a business case and talk to and influence the usual stakeholders. At some stage in the selling process the changemaker will be asked, 'What do you think of solutions A, B and C, what's your advice?'

Changemakers are often involved in the buying process, but often they are not. Don't forget their natural habitat is online. So just as we will make a decision to stay at a hotel by looking on TripAdvisor, they may be making decisions based on what they see online.

Influence marketing

We can see that influence marketing will grow in its use by brands and suppliers. Television has limited reach as people watch more YouTube videos and stream more content. It is now easier for some brands and marketers to pay a blogger/vlogger money to promote a product, or to give their product to an English Premier League footballer, than it is to create an ad and buy ad space.

In addition, ads online are getting cleverer. The fact that you can drop a cookie on somebody's computer, follow them around the sites they visit, and then present targeted ads, is something that more and more people will look into. That is, on the basis that the cost of the technology will reduce. In the past you purchased an ad in a magazine and hoped that somebody would look at it. Now when your prospects look at certain things online you can present them with an ad for your product and service. We have all looked for a hotel, then gone onto Facebook and been presented with ads for another hotel chain in the side bar on the right.

As we mention in this book, influence comes in many forms, and the large companies such as Gartner, Accenture, etc will always provide influence. But we will see a further rise of the online influencer and 'smaller' online influencer.

Influence can be very 'David and Goliath', and the Goliath influencers will still be out there: the social media celebrities – we all know who they are. In addition, there will also be the social media 'Davids' who may be relevant for your niche, target market or the message you want to get across.

Sometimes the influence may extend to a particular social network platform. You may be targeting people and a Snapchat influencer will fit the market and age group you are looking at.

Brands still cling to the belief that the employee brand advocacy programme is great as you can control the message by telling people what to tweet. But if you want more reach and influence you need to let go of the leash on the employees and open up to influencers. You may not be able to control the message, but you will get more reach and amplification for your dollar.

Brands and suppliers do have to become more sophisticated about influence marketing. Currently sophistication levels are pretty low, with it not being very different from old-school advertising, sales events or product placement. Often this is because people don't understand how to harness influence, or they use old world/analogue techniques in a digital world.

Brands also have to understand that sometimes it doesn't work. A brand once gave us free phones, and when we used them we didn't like them. Obviously, the actual cost to the supplier of the phone was relatively low, but it did mean there was a major impact for that supplier.

How the marketing mix changes

We are not saying you should move everything into one area. Marketing has, and always will be about a mix of activities. We are saying that you need to move your marketing budget where your customers are, and that's online.

At this point you need to experiment and find what works for you. In this age of disruption, all the old assumptions we made about business are up for re-evaluation. Yes, all of them. What worked in 2010 may not work now and what we tried in 1980 may work now. Why not send letters to people – it might be a bit different?

But you will need to mix things up online. Buying a position on a podcast or a banner ad is probably a bit obvious. You are aware that you are more likely to be struck by lightning than to click on a banner ad. But you could buy some tweets with an influencer, or pay to guest-post on their blog.

Creating content is just about sitting down and finding the time to write that content. There are enough channels, probably too many, in which to distribute it.

But is anybody listening? That is why we wrote about the need for community and not just followers so early in the book. This is such an important investment and asset for a company. As we said, community is NOT an e-mail list, it is an active network of people sharing and amplifying ideas and content. They will be your prospects, customers, advocates and influencers all working together to drive your brand's success.

Note: I've said prospects, as there is no reason why people who haven't purchased won't be ready to buy from you when their time is right.

Social maturity – ramping up quicker

In Chapter 9 on social maturity, we go through the steps that a company needs to take to move from being an analogue business to being a digital one. We argue that there are no short cuts; there needs to be an organic growth of social in an organization, and you cannot just decide to be social by command and control.

That said, many companies need to accelerate their way through the steps and the only way you can manage any change programme that needs different processes and behaviours is by training.

We see so many companies 'doing' social, when really they are just 'spinning their wheels' and wasting their time while their competitors overtake them.

Training must be top down and this means that the senior management must lead by example.

We see so many opportunities for CEOs of organizations to explain to the world their company's story and brand. You only have to look at the number of Richard Branson quotes that are shared online. We wonder sometimes, did he actually ever say them? But it doesn't matter; we have inspirational quotes posted by people who have nothing to do with his brands, and this is free advertising.

There are many more inspirational CEOs out there than the few we see quoted. Getting the message across is pretty simple. Just think of the (revenue) impact it would make if your CEO's leadership and inspiration was visible and being shared?

We agree that you run the risk of producing navel-gazing management consulting speak that is full of jargon. But isn't that the point of employing and nurturing people that understand social, have the relevant business acumen and are able to stand up to the internal forces that don't actually 'get' social but think they do?

One of the reasons we came up with the maturity model was so that companies can benchmark themselves as to where they are. Senior executives who might not really 'get' social can spot the symptoms or effects of what is being played back in their organization. We have seen people in organizations get prizes for tweeting the most or for creating initiatives based on something like Klout.

There used to be a health and safety video in the UK about the dangers of swimming in the sea. The video explained to the layperson why they needed to be careful about being swept out to sea, but it also explained what a person should do, firstly to recognize that somebody was drowning, but what to do to save them.

These random acts of social are like watching a drowning person thrash around in the sea. First, organizations need to understand that random acts of social don't help you. In the health and safety video, a passer-by thinks the drowning person is waving at them and just waves back. Random acts of social are not about how you are progressing – you are drowning.

You need to recognize this and throw somebody a lifeline.

We have seen people running initiatives using Klout as a measure. Whatever you think about Klout, it's a measurement for use across multiple (LinkedIn, Facebook, Instagram, etc) platforms. In that same organization, we are training people in how to send their first tweet and debating if there is a copyright on images found on Google and whether you can use them for tweets.

Taking the organization together for all disciplines and skill sets is critical. Random acts of social just put people off and they just mentally 'pull up the drawbridge' and switch off.

Technology future

In the world of digital we have many small and large technology firms fighting over licences or, in the world of Cloud, subscriptions, that offer us better ways of marketing. In the world of digital marketing there are few 'suites' of products but instead a list of tools that need a sticking plaster to bring them together. You can buy marketing systems, sales systems, e-mail systems, web systems, and social media listening.

Digital marketing has provided businesses with a step change in marketing best practice. While terms such as MQLs (Marketing Qualified Leads), BQLs (Business Qualified Leads), and SQLs (Sales Qualified Leads) do increase the amount of terminology, which isn't good, they do help to define what a lead is, and for us salespeople they define how a lead is qualified, and so how likely it is to turn into revenue. This is a major step forward.

Those business cards that people used to come back from conferences with, which sales would just put in the bin, are now MQLs. Usually marketing, through an outside agency or an inside sales team, will qualify them. This will weed out the people who won't buy anything from you, such as students looking for white papers for a thesis etc. They may well buy something from you in the future, though, and they are more likely to do this if you treat them nicely and send them the white paper, rather than just putting the request in the bin.

Then, once an inside sales team has sifted through the MQLs and turned them into BQLs (usually with authority and need from BANT), the sales can go through the BQLs and are accepted as SQLs.

BANT = Budget, Authority, Need and Timescales.

Lack of relevance of BANT

A note on BANT: we are seeing in the world of Cloud that BANT is becoming redundant as a lead qualification methodology.

In the past, sales teams would qualify an account based on the fact that you were talking to somebody with a 'need' who had 'authority'. Sales managers and sales training would always insist that a salesperson ask the customer or prospect, 'what is the budget?' The customer would say yes, they had a budget, whether they did or they didn't. They knew that if they said they didn't have a budget the salesperson would get in their car and drive away. The salesperson was always taught to ask when the customer would buy. That is, what month or week, etc, enabling the salesperson to fill in the fields in the CRM systems.

We are now seeing – especially in the world of digital selling, which is often being driven by SaaS (software as a service) vendors – that if you wait for the customer to have a budget and timescale you have lost the business. Or that you are in a price war with a competitor that drives down your margins.

Salespeople now, using digital as well as their own selling skills, can work with the customer or prospect to create a business case. Any vendor that has been through the last few recessions will have created an ROI tool in some shape or format. Now while a customer won't always believe a vendor's ROI figures – sometimes they can read a bit like the Immaculate Conception – they will want to work with a partner.

Any B2B purchase will require some change to go with it, and customers will want to understand how it will impact their organization; the people, the process, the technology and the risks. Customers will want to know how you implemented before, where it went wrong and where it went right.

Customers are far too wise for suppliers to hide where things went wrong. Everybody knows that any programme of change will hit 'turbulence', but what customers want to know is how you managed it and what they can do to mitigate those risks.

So when you read that the modern salesperson needs to 'add value' to the customer, this is what is meant. You should be able to articulate the steps the customers need to go through to gain the benefits they are planning for. Part of this may be teaching them new concepts, for example, in Cloud the lack of reliance on the internal IT department.

That is why BANT is no longer relevant. You must be working with the customer on the budget and business case and you must work with the client on the timescales.

Close plans are dead

We are seeing, in the organizations that understand customer experience, that they have killed off the close plan.

The close plan was always of the making of the salesperson. I don't ever remember a customer coming to us and saying, 'Let's put together a close plan'.

The close plan was always about what steps the customer organization needed to put together to help the salesperson close the deal. If the customer had come across this before they might build into it the first kick-off meeting in which there was a handover to the delivery team. Or better still the customer would ask for a meeting with the delivery team before signing so they could see if there was a meeting of minds.

The close plan was how sales would get the relevant paperwork, purchase order, and signed contract, and then once that paperwork was in the salesperson's hand, you never saw them again. Or you only saw them when it was time for a renewal or they wanted a reference for the next sale.

Customers are now more demanding and salespeople need to wake up to this, and offer a go-live plan proactively. That is, customer and salesperson work back from the go-live date, through the requirements for the project over the various project stages.

This requires salespeople to share what is required, internally and externally (maybe consultants are needed), and provide a realistic project timeframe.

While salespeople may look at this and think, 'I don't want my customer to understand the change and risks they will meet', what it does provide to the salesperson is competitive advantage over late-stage entrants. We are not saying that clients will do this with you exclusively – we would normally expect they would do it with the final shortlist of two. But there again, they might take you through this as a preferred supplier.

It does bond you closer to the client and gives you your close plan but in a more customer-friendly/ongoing supportive partnership way.

Often we have seen this work well when salespeople have built renewals or reference/advocate milestones into it. 'If we do this for you, will you do X reference calls/meetings?' It often works well when implementation timeframes are tight and you can demonstrate to the client, for example, that they need to go to the March rather than the April board meeting.

As we say above, this does not guarantee you success, but there may be competitors out there listening to what you and your customers are doing. Then this is a great method to lock out any late entrants, especially if they know they are late and just try to 'burn the deal down' with a very low price.

Social selling as a software suite

We are being contacted all the time about influencer solutions, LinkedIn solutions, etc.

In the future we are looking for companies to create a go-to-market around social selling. That is, a set of software solutions that are sold to salespeople to support social selling: selling in a digital world. We are not just talking about a CRM (customer relationship management) system here that just holds names and addresses, but a solution that will support a company's internal digital sales initiative.

Of course, this may not cover everything – there will be a requirement for links to other mobile apps or companies such as LinkedIn – but it would be a 'stake in the ground' and show the major IT companies that if they do this, they understand digital. Without it, we think it shows they don't.

It would also mean that the social selling industry would have research and development dollars going into looking at how to use digital technologies to sell, rather than the investment dollars that currently go into how we market.

Please don't do what the exec said to me: 'Let's automate social media and go back to doing our day jobs'. Automation is probably one of the best tools we can use, but at the same time, the very worst.

So many times I sit in meetings and people ask me, 'Can you tell me which tool I can use so I can come in on a Monday and create my tweets so I can hit my KPI for the week?'

Hopefully, having read this book you will understand that social is now part of our daily lives and processes. This isn't about doing a bit of digital, getting a 'tick in the box' with our KPI and going back to doing work as we did.

Digital selling requires a different mindset, an online mindset, and this means tweeting, informing and teaching. Like we always did, but online. Random acts of social just confuse everybody and often let senior management off the hook. This really is about a change in working as we move from the industrial age to the digital age.

Conclusion

We wish you luck, but with this book, you shouldn't need it!

Matt and Tim are always keen to connect and hear about your journeys – what is working, what isn't working. Please share with us your best practice; we'd be happy to keep this confidential or maybe even write a blog or interview you on a webcast.

Don't forget you can also access more bonus downloadable material at: **www.koganpage.com/socialselling**

If you'd prefer to get in touch directly, please do come over and say hello on Twitter: **@timothy_hughes** and **@mbrit**

Good luck and happy selling!
Tim and Matt

REFERENCES

Keltner, D (2012) The compassionate species, *Greater Good* [online] http://greatergood.berkeley.edu/article/item/the_compassionate_species

Knoblauch, M (2014) Millennials trust user-generated content 50% more than other media, *Mashable* [online] http://mashable.com/2014/04/09/millennials-user-generated-media/#Bvohe6t8YgqD

Levy, H (2015) The economics of connections, *Gartner* [online] http://www.gartner.com/smarterwithgartner/the-economics-of-connections/

Office for National Statistics (2015) Five facts about online retail sales in the UK, *National Archives* [online] http://www.ons.gov.uk/ons/rel/rdit2/e-commerce-and-internet-use/5-facts-relating-to-web-sales/sty-5-facts.html

Shirky, Clay (2008) It's not information load. It's filter failure, *YouTube* [online] https://www.youtube.com/watch?v=LabqeJEOQyI&feature=youtu.be

Tuomisto-Inch, H (2015) Digital tipping points for 2015, *Slideshare* [online] http://www.slideshare.net/JamesSmee1/digital-tipping-points-for-2015

INDEX

Note: *italics* indicate a Figure or Table in the text.

CPSIA information can be obtained
at www.ICGtesting.com
Printed in the USA
JSHW021943301220
10594JS00007B/129